THE CREATIVE FEMININE AND
HER DISCONTENTS

THE CREATIVE FEMININE AND HER DISCONTENTS

PSYCHOTHERAPY, ART, AND DESTRUCTION

Juliet Miller

KARNAC

First published in 2008 by
Karnac Books Ltd
118 Finchley Road, London NW3 5HT

Copyright © 2008 Juliet Miller

The right of Juliet Miller to be identified as the author of this work has been asserted in accordance with §§ 77 and 78 of the Copyright Design and Patents Act 1988.

British Library Cataloguing in Publication Data

A C.I.P. for this book is available from the British Library

ISBN 978 1 85575 555 0

Cover image: "The Fruits of the Earth", 1938, oil on canvas by Frida Kahlo, reproduced with permission of Instituto Nacional de Bellas Artes and Banco de Mexico. Collection Banco Nacional de Mexico, Mexico. Index/The Bridgeman Art Library.

Edited, designed and produced by The Studio Publishing Services Ltd
www.studiopublishingservicesuk.co.uk
e-mail: studio@publishingservicesuk.co.uk

Printed in Great Britain

10 9 8 7 6 5 4 3 2 1

www.karnacbooks.com

CONTENTS

For Katharine and Olga

ACKNOWLEDGEMENTS

I am very grateful to Cornelia Parker and Louise Bourgeois for their kind permission to reproduce images of their work. I also wish to thank Dale McFarland at The Frith Street Gallery and Wendy Williams at Bourgeois Studio for their time and help.

My thanks to Banco de Mexico and Instituto Nacional de Bellas Artes y Literatura for permission to reproduce "My Birth" and "Fruits of the Earth", by Frida Kahlo and to The Bridgeman Art Library.

Thanks also to the Museo Poldi Pezzoli, Milan, for permission to reproduce "The Virgin and the Child", sometimes known as "The Virgin Teaching the Infant Jesus to Read", by Alessandro Botticelli, and to The Bridgeman Art Library.

My thanks to the publishers HarperCollins and Hodder and Stoughton, respectively, for permission to include an extract from *Bad Blood*, by Lorna Sage, and an extract from *What I Loved*, by Siri Hustvedt.

To my patients I owe a debt of gratitude for helping me to understand, and for their generous permission to refer to their stories.

I am indebted to my women friends for their interest and ideas, and especially to the following for their ongoing support and encouragement: Penny Kegerreis, Josephine King, Polly Macdonald, Julia

Rickett, Janey Stevens, and Mary Travis. Diane Hirst generously shared her editorial expertise and her creativity. David Arnold, as always, offered his rich experience of writing and his invaluable common sense.

Chapter Eight was originally published in 2005 as "Explode, stretch and squash. Creative destruction in the work of Cornelia Parker", in *Harvest International Journal for Jungian Studies*, 51(2).

An earlier version of Chapter Two was originally published in 2005 as "Playing with fire. Sounds, secrets and singing", in *Harvest International Journal of Jungian Studies*, 51(1).

Chapter Seven was first given in an earlier form as a paper, "I do, I undo, I redo", to The Independent Group of Analytical Psychologists in May 2006.

Juliet Miller is a Jungian analyst with a private practice in London. Prior to training as an analyst, she worked as a documentary film maker on environmental, social, and women's issues. She is especially interested in creative expression and the interface between the arts and psychotherapy. She is co-editor with Jane Haynes of *Inconceivable Conceptions. Psychological Aspects of Infertility and Reproductive Technology*. Brunner-Routledge (2003).

INTRODUCTION

The idea for this book was born out of a fascination with the creative process in all its different manifestations, but primarily from a desire to understand aspects of my own relationship to creativity that had often seemed problematic and elusive. Over the years, this creative energy would occasionally flow, but more often than not it seemed to stumble and stop, and then the capacity to make or write or paint became submerged and sometimes lost. The strong desire to create did not appear to be enough to make it happen, and a struggle with myself, sometimes quite prolonged, would ensue. But what was this struggle about and why did it seem to be necessary?

When I became a psychotherapist, I recognized that my own experiences around creativity were coming up in a similar way for my female patients, who also appeared to be frequently thwarted in their creative endeavours. Their questions about the frustration and rage that they had to negotiate in the process of creating did not seem to emerge in a similar way for the men that I worked with. It appeared that there might be specific issues for women around aspects of their creativity that were not true for the men.

These questions for women did not seem to be easily answered by the theoretical background that I had been trained in. The language of psychotherapy and psychoanalysis was not open or flexible enough to be able to explore these questions fully; rather, it often felt restricting in what it could imagine and represent for the feminine psyche.

This book, then, is an attempt to look at creativity from a female perspective. It is an exploration of what these specific difficulties for women might be and how we might think about them and try to find a way through them. I am aware that men also experience difficulties with their creative selves, but I believe the problems are significantly different ones, and not ones that I look at here. I do, however, address the fact that we all suffer, men and women, if women feel cut off from important aspects of their internal creative lives. If aspects of the creative feminine appear inaccessible to women, then they are also not available to men, and this is a double tragedy.

Although the book is written from the perspective of a Jungian analyst, primarily interested in the life of the psyche, I also examine some of the historical, cultural, and social reasons why women may have specific issues relating to their creativity. Together, I suggest, these all add up to a multi-layered and conflicted mixture of barriers and fears for women who wish to express themselves. I explore women's subjective experiences of their creative selves as writers, singers, mothers, therapists, and artists, and argue that these subjective experiences are marginalized by the symbolism and language that is available to express and explore the creative feminine. It is a premise of this book that one of the problems about writing or speaking about female creativity is that the language of a patriarchal world is restricted to speaking *about* women and not *for* them.

I question how procreativity and maternity affect women's creativity, and how having bodies that make babies may make it more difficult for women to express themselves in other creative ways. I look at how expectations of maternity restrict women's own multi-faceted experiences of mothering. I also look at how women's expectations of relating may get in the way of their creativity, and suggest that women who are infertile may be able to contact shadow aspects of motherhood that highlight dark but crucial sides of the creative feminine.

By looking at some of the relationships between female analysts and female patients with the psychoanalytic founding fathers, Jung and Freud, I highlight ways in which the therapeutic profession has continued to emulate these early mistakes of patriarchy in the profession. By looking at analytic training institutes and their defensive and insular methods, I explore how an inherited fear and hatred of the creative feminine is perpetuated. I argue that this has become part of the theory and structure of the profession.

Finally, I step outside the whole of psychotherapy and consider the work of two contemporary women sculptors, Louise Bourgeois and Cornelia Parker. I assess what they can show us about new and authentic relationships to creativity through ideas of deconstruction and reconstruction in their work. In two very different ways, both these artists show us how the expression of aggression, sadism, and destruction are crucial to an authentic expression of the feminine self.

Many of the writers to whom I refer are Jungian analysts or psychotherapists. But I also refer to the work of Freudian psychoanalysts, lawyers, novelists, artists, feminists, and sociologists, who are all separately identified in the text. Within the psychotherapeutic world there is a very small body of work on female creativity, and I am indebted to that written by Marion Milner, Rosemary Gordon, and Marion Woodman. There is an increasing body of more recent work by post Jungians on female identity, and I refer widely to that by Polly Young-Eisendrath, Tessa Adams, Andrea Duncan, and Sue Austin. This book attempts to build on their work and to place women's problematic relationships to their creativity into a similar area worthy of questioning and debate both within and outside the profession.

PART I
CREATIVITY AND FEAR

CHAPTER ONE

The search for a voice

"Women have been in darkness for centuries. They don't know themselves. Or only poorly. And when women write, they translate this darkness. . . . The writing of women is really translating from the unknown, like a new way of communicating, rather than an already formed language"

(Duras, 1975)

A life lived creatively comes in many forms, from the day to day pleasures taken in the rhythms and changes of inner and outer worlds to the artistically creative person who needs to create and make things as both a journey of discovery and a reason for living. The former may entail a creative capacity to simply *be* and let go of the pressures and demands of modern life. The latter is initially a more active state requiring an engagement with creative energies and drives. It is the ways in which some women find it difficult to relate to these creative drives that I shall be writing about. In this chapter I give an overview and look at how the areas of symbolism, language, and patriarchy affect women's abilities to express themselves creatively, and how fear and rage may dominate when they are attempting to find their *own* voice.

There is a seminal moment from my own youth, which encapsulates some of the issues that I am exploring. When I was about thirteen years old, my father, in an attempt to encourage what he saw as my drive and determination, said, "When you are older you'll make a very good secretary to some high up and important man." My immediate reaction was one of fury: "I don't want to be the secretary, I want to be the important man." Within the culture of the late 1950s, when Britain was deep in the grey wasteland that was post war recovery, this was, in retrospect, quite an enlightened comment for my father to have made. However, it is the first time I can remember expressing the rage I felt at being seen by my father as *less than* a man. Now it also interests me that I was not able to express that I wanted to be an important *woman*; it was as if I felt imprisoned in a male language that had no imagery to express my female desires.

The need to be in an ongoing and strong relationship with my own creativity has been a central drive of my life so far. I do not believe that my experience can be subsumed entirely into an overall experience of the relationship of human beings to their creative selves, but that this struggle has aspects that are gender specific, and that men and women do form an image of their creativity differently. I see my own struggle to express myself creatively as weighed down with cultural and archetypal significances that bring with them a profound sense of doing wrong. As a result, the expression of my creativity as a woman can feel like an expression of disobedience and, sometimes, also a destructive act. The sense of disobedience may come about as the result of stepping out of accepted ways of being. The feelings of destruction are, I believe, central to acts of creation, and also represent shadow aspects of femininity that may be difficult but crucial for women to own.

As a psychotherapist I know that this struggle to find a creative voice holds true for many of my female patients. The anxiety and fear generated by this struggle can be just as intense as it was for women fifty or a hundred years ago. This is despite extensive feminist scholarship and the many important social advances that have opened up the world to women. It is now possible for women to belong to the working world of men in many different ways and to have independent lives and careers of their own. However, this acceptance into a patriarchal world has not helped to access a feminine creativity but has rather encouraged a sense of being able to slip unnoticed into the privileged male position. Some of my patients who work in the extraverted worlds of business or the media suffer from intense competitive anxiety that may isolate them from their creative feminine resources. They may be thwarted by exhaustion and rage and the need to adopt hard personas to survive. Or, alternatively, if they have decided to stay at home with children, they may feel themselves drawn into a singular and unchangeable domestic identity arranged around children's and partner's needs.

It can seem as if very little has changed in our social and cultural views of women and their creative needs when *Mslexia*, the magazine for women who write, has regular features on ideas for preserving space both psychically and concretely within the family home. Some of these suggestions appear simplistic, "sleep less', "pay a cleaner', "give up leisure time', yet any of these might be big steps to take for a woman who feels that her roles are primarily as mother or as wage earner and that her creativity always has to come second (Taylor, 2004, p. 13). Some of my patients feel that there are only two options available for women to take, neither of which feels right: to be passive about their creative losses, or to take on the fight with *men*. To play the subservient role and swallow the rage and anger can damage one's relationship to the self, and this is not fertile ground for creative expression. However, to take on the battle with patriarchy can be a dangerous game that can involve sacrifice on a deep level and can produce similarly infertile ground. This dichotomy is reflected and supported by the available imagery and symbolism that reflects women's psychic lives.

Our culture is replete with religious and symbolic images of women that are either subservient or sacrificial and that do not hold and reflect the multiplicities of women's creative powers. The Virgin Mary may be fertile and maternal, but she is also a passive figure who exists only in relation to the male God and cannot be freed from her role as handmaiden. Mary remains both detached from the realities of womankind and idealized in her supporting role, despite the attempts by the Catholic Church to deify her through her Assumption into Heaven.

> The image of the Virgin Mary perpetuates the split between soul
> and body, passivity and activity. It leaves men powerful, and
> untroubled by her body, which they have eliminated. It exemplifies
> what is lacking for women, while at the same time attempting to fill
> the lack with an image of woman as divine. [Clark, 2003, p. 201]

Seeing woman as "divine" simply exacerbates the problem by displacing her into the cosmos when she should be firmly rooted on the ground where she can participate fully in the world.

Images of sacrificial women are also deeply embedded in our Western Judaic-Christian tradition. Eve, the first woman, took on the battle with patriarchy and disobeyed God: "Of every tree of the garden thou mayest freely eat: but of the tree of the knowledge of good and evil, thou shalt not eat of it: for in the day that thou eatest thereof thou shalt surely die" (Genesis 2: 16–17). There have been many modern attempts to reinterpret Eve's act of disobedience by attempting to separate her from the image of feminine evil, which is an impossible legacy for western women to carry. Judith Hubback suggests that, by disobeying God, Eve was laying the foundations for developing her own inner law and truthfulness to herself, although the punishment for gaining this knowledge was to be cast out of Paradise (Hubback, 1993, p. 5). Helena Kennedy, the feminist lawyer, has come to the even stronger conclusion that "Eve was framed", that she was made to take the rap for men's sexual and violent appetites (Kennedy, 1993, p. 12). The most optimistic reading of the Eve myth is that through her disobedience she was instrumental in making our conscious world (Ross, 1993, p. xii). In this reading we are encouraged to see Eve as a source of powerful creative energy, a woman who was capable of making the world as we know it, although still burdened with the guilt of disobedience. This image of Eve as disobedient to God has, however, to bear the weight of carrying the fear of the feminine as promulgated by the Church with its need to keep the feminine unconscious and evil.

It is now widely acknowledged by many feminists and psychotherapists that our Western religious images cannot be reinterpreted or moulded to give women in the twenty-first century an appropriate new symbolic language, as these images do not make for living and creative feminine images but, rather, psychically static ones. Re-examining these Western religious images is simply one of the ways in which women are scouring cultures and reinterpreting the symbolic in an attempt to create a space and a language for the exploration of female identity and creativity. There is work going on which searches backwards for creative and vibrant female images within the Greek myths (Baring & Cashford, 1993; Shearer, 1996) and within stories and myths in pre-industrial cultures (Culbert-Koehn, 2002). In an attempt to discover multi-faceted women or goddesses who also embrace and respect shadow aspects of femininity, psychotherapists have looked to the East. "Kali's power to rage symbolizes the power many women need to develop in themselves—the power to assert themselves, to set their limits, to say no when necessary" (Leonard, 1998, p. 123). Recent work on nineteenth and twentieth century literature has been sourced for new and positive interpretations of women that cut across cultural expectations (Duncan, 2003a). All this work has helped to highlight the lack of available and vibrant images that can be called into play when thinking about the creative feminine.

Alongside and interwoven with this search for images is the ongoing work that is examining language as an androcentric structure, a language that accepts the male viewpoint as "the truth" and that can only therefore speak *about* rather than *for* women. This means that there is an ongoing problem in talking about "the creative feminine", as there is no universal female reality that can be taken as read, except for the culturally institutionalized one of reading women as lacking in relation to men. It is problematic, also, that this baseline has unfortunately been one of the foundations for modern psychoanalytic and psychotherapeutic work. The difficulty of being a female psychotherapist or a female patient is to be confronted daily with the issues of being "less than", within a theoretical and professional framework that rarely questions this.

> As a psychotherapist I have been faced repeatedly with theories of female inadequacy—theories like penis envy or the inferior moral and intellectual capacity of women—that arise from the assumption that the female person is inherently lacking something. Once a woman is seen as inherently lacking, then one can reason that she is just "naturally" depressed, enraged, or compensating for this inadequacy. [Young-Eisendrath, 2004, p. 94]

Much psychoanalytic writing has been androcentric in its perspective. To be aware of this is not a simple process where it is good enough to have a conscious feminist outlook, where difference is respected rather than marginalized. It also means that there is an ongoing struggle to explore and communicate because of the lack of symbols and meanings around the idea of a creative feminine life, apart, of course, from those myriad ones associated with procreation and nurturing (the most widely accepted and symbolized form of female creativity).

It is crucial, therefore, not to assume, which much psychoanalytic writing has done, that gender and sexual differences inevitably go together; that the feminine inevitably means the female person and the masculine inevitably means the male. In fact, to use these words "feminine" and "masculine" means that we can easily become trapped by identifications and images whilst every reader, female or male brings to the reading a different reality. It can also become difficult to see the similarities rather than the differences and to acknowledge the things that men and women share; that they both suffer from the image of the female as "less than" and from the wounding and suppression of the feminine.

This suppression of the feminine is so much a part of our cultural, historical, and psychological histories that we are frequently blind to it and, as Young-Eisendrath suggests, it forms a benchmark that traps women and pathologizes their "unfeminine" emotions. Working psychologically with women, I am often confronted with layer upon layer of defensive structure against, and fear of, the expression of their creativity. Ideas of why it is so hard for them might start with complaints about not being good enough, or narcissistic desires for perfection, but if it is possible to explore beneath these fears there are deeper ones about what would happen to them if they allowed their creativity to flow. Sometimes these fears can be understood as fears of doing better than the parents, or guilt at toppling the parents from their superior position. However, these generational fears may also be experienced by the men I see in my practice. The women, however, often eventually express a terror at being seen to be creative. They seem to feel that they will be giving up a safe identity for a dangerous new one; an identity within which they will no longer be accepted, or one where they fear to be seen as mad or as disobeying every expectation of gender and society. This would be an entirely new identity, where they relate first to themselves rather than primarily to others, and one where an element of forcefulness and aggression was essential.

In Germaine Greer's *The Obstacle Race,* her extensive rediscovery of women painters of the past four hundred years, she comes to the conclusion that this fear of a new identity is central to women's inability to fully enter the world of art and that, as a result, the women artists she writes about conformed, copied, and subverted their natural abilities.

> For all artists the problem is one of finding one's own authenticity, of speaking in a language or imagery that is essentially one's own, but if one's self image is dictated by one's relation to others and all one's activities are other—directed, it is simply not possible to find one's own voice. [Greer, 1979, p. 325]

Some of my patients who struggle to write are made anxious by the idea of being published and, therefore, what ideas and feelings will suddenly be in the public domain. This domain is frequently the small scale one inhabited by relatives or friends, and the anxiety is about how *they* will react to the published work rather than how it will be received by the general public. The fear of being seen as disobedient and stepping out of role may be because the writing reveals that the author has thoughts about sex and aggression that she has kept silent about to close family members. This can be a more powerful restriction on women's creativity than any concern about the value of the work in the wider world.

For a new identity to become safe it has to be inhabited and lived, and if this new identity means revealing to the world the strength of your feelings and your desires that you have done your utmost to keep hidden all your life, this can feel like an enormous risk to take. Allowing your creativity to be seen may change some fundamental close relationships forever. The envy of others may feel like too high a price to pay for some women, who fear losing closeness and relatedness. For some women, to show their creativity can feel very dangerous. When I first had a paper published in a professional journal, a colleague, who also wrote, warned me sadly, "Now you will know what it is like to put your head above the parapet!"

It may be safer to continue to identify with the expectation that your role is primarily one of relating to others, and so project your feared creativity on to another to hold for you. The chosen one may be a controlling or bullying man, and this may suit the woman perfectly if she wishes to continue to see the aggression as belonging to the other rather than herself. If a woman is consciously aware of her struggle to express herself it can be hard for her to appreciate how self destructive she may be in relation to her own creativity. For some women, their masochism (which I suggest is a result of the accepted theory of female inadequacy) is so deeply embedded in their way of being that they cannot identify this as a problem; it is part of their being. Wounding the self is often used by women as the preferred and more controlled way of expressing their aggression. It may be a deeply held belief that this matters less in the scheme of things than bearing the unknown results of expressing their anger or forcefulness towards another.

The passivity involved in taking this position can leave a woman feeling that she is unable to know what she wants or feels, or even, in extreme cases, that her feelings are irrelevant to her. Some women express that they do not know what I am talking about when I mention their creativity. They may feel that they do not have the tools to think about themselves in this way. As I have suggested above, this may be literally true in the sense of having no accepted language or symbols to form an image of a feminine creative self.

In 1934, the psychoanalyst Marion Milner, in her detailed exploration of how she put unconscious blocks in the way of her own creativity and happiness, came to the conclusion that if she did not develop and explore what she called her "male" capacity for thinking, she was lost. She discovered that there was an aspect of her self-experience that she had not been acknowledging as belonging to her. Milner realized that she needed to embrace these characteristics rather than seeing them as a problem.

> So my discovery of a natural rhythm of awareness was perhaps the discovery that reflective thinking requires a subtle balance of male and female activity. Was it not true, or at least useful, to say that as long as I remained all female in my thinking I was passive towards it, leaving it to think itself, unexpressed and unwatched . . . [Milner, 1952, p. 217]

Milner is naming her capacity for active thinking here as the *male* activity, the one that brings the thought into the world. Writing within the contexts of her time, she named these repressed parts of herself as the *male* ones. We might think of these now as appropriate *female* characteristics to own rather than as picturing them as male or projecting them on to men.

A capacity to stand apart from, as well as to be inside, the suffering generated by an androcentric world or one dominated by patriarchal values is not a comfortable or easy thing to do. Marion Milner's account of her self-analysis is laborious and taxing. However, Milner, I believe, was struggling with a central theme of *this* book, that for a woman to get in touch with her creativity it is crucial that she confronts the daimon of destruction and aggression. This daimon is not *only* an external stultifying force to be reckoned with but also a powerful internal one, which can wreak havoc with creative abilities if it is not acknowledged and accepted by a woman as part of herself.

> . . . it is vital for women to face up to their aggression, including their capacity to be sadistic towards others. Only once we acknowledge that aspect of our personalities will we be able to draw on this "masculine" forcefulness and use it creatively to fight for personal and political equality. [Maguire, 2004, p. 116]

Mary Maguire is here suggesting that owning aggression is part of the feminist agenda. I believe it is also directly related to a woman's capacity to be creative.

Women patients often spend time raging against the injustices of the world, and feel that any attempt on the part of the therapist to look at the destruction that is being waged internally is the same as colluding with the brutal father or brother or husband and that they would be abandoning them, just as they feel previous close relationships have done. It is this external concretizing of the internal struggle that can make it especially difficult for women. There is already a powerful external reality of misogyny and brutality that many of them have had to face and it is not surprising that there may be a strong desire for a peaceful internal world. However, it can also be very liberating for women to discover that they are allowed to have violent and destructive thoughts and to be able to link these to, and accept them as an essential part of, their creative selves.

Jung's work has been sourced as creative fuel for the contemporary feminine agenda, and yet his writings have also held it back. His extensive work on the feminine reflected the cultural and social mores of his time in that he saw women's roles as "in relation" to men, and their creative capacities often as simply reflecting his own anima projections. (I explore this weakness of Jung's thinking and its effects on the early days of psychoanalysis in a later chapter.) Jung's work on archetypes, however, was revolutionary, and has spawned much post-Jungian work on the potential for a sexual duality for men and women within the idea of the androgynous archetype (Samuels, 1993, p. 146). This capacity of the archetype to be androgynous, whether experienced or expressed through a man or a woman, has been of major importance in post-Jungian work on feminine identities and has helped to open up a more fluid approach to an understanding of the suppressed potentialities of "the feminine".

A Jungian understanding of archetypes in terms of opposites is also of importance to the thesis of this book. For instance, writing of the conflicts and tensions inherent in the creative archetype, Jung saw it as having a daimon. The daimon is the power to destroy that is inextricably attached to the power to create. Much of the thinking around this was developed from the innovative thinking on creativity and destruction by a female patient and colleague of Jung's, Sabina Spielrein, whose work I consider in a later chapter. She was the first of the psychoanalysts to understand that to bring something new into being something else has to be destroyed. This understanding of the destructive power of creativity is also essential to an understanding of why women may have specific problems, and is a theme fully explored in the last section of the book, which is about two female sculptors.

The tension within the creative archetype (as in all archetypes) was also paralleled in the much documented relationship between Jung and Freud. Jung, the younger man, was initially seen by Freud as the messenger for his own psychoanalytic project into the next generation, until this expectation died through Jung's determination to carve out his own field of psychoanalysis. There is an interesting example of the tension between the two men and of their differing views of the creative drive in Deidre Bair's biography of Jung. Here she describes their confrontation over the alleged story of Amenophis IV, who destroyed all his father's regal cartouches (his name wherever it appeared officially): "Jung 'irritated to the extreme'" (because of Freud's belief that Jung was acting out his father complex by trying to take over his mantle) "immediately interjected that the pharaoh had done so, 'not as an act of resistance against his father but because he was a creative man'" (Bair, 2004, p. 236). This statement affected Freud so deeply that he passed out. Bair suggests that Freud was somatizing his fear that Jung was capable of seizing his own intellectual mantle. Freud experienced Jung's creative drive as destructive against himself rather than as a necessary creative act on Jung's part. It probably depends from which side of the ideological battle you view this story, as to which end of the archetype appears utmost. However, Bair does show how the destructive power of creativity cannot be underestimated and is unconsciously feared.

The creative daimon, in the violence of its need to express itself through the person, is clearly not gender specific, and can be experienced as profoundly destructive and frightening for men also. Henri Matisse put himself (or was put) through physical and mental torture every time he attempted to break through to a new level in his painting. He described this shattering experience as a rape of himself by painting's demands and a rupturing of his relational needs:

> I reckon I've made progress when I recognize more and more clearly in my work a detachment from the support offered by the model (the presence of the model, who is there not so much to provide possible information about her physical constitution as to keep me in a state of emotion, a sort of flirtation which ends by turning into a rape. Whose rape? A rape of myself, of a certain tenderness or weakening in face of a sympathetic object). [Spurling, 2005, p. 24]

In her biography of Matisse, the biographer Hilary Spurling makes a strong case for Matisse's life-long restraint against having sex with his models. She argues that if he had acted out this rape scenario by allowing himself to be seduced by the model, the painting would have lost its fire. It was crucial that the experience of rape had to be an internal experience of his creative relationship with painting as *she*. That this is a symbolic rape, brought on by the power of the creative daimon, does nothing to reduce its force or terror. It frequently culminated, for Matisse, in severe illness, panic attacks, insomnia, and a resulting isolation from his family. It is interesting that these regular and dramatic internal terrors, stimulated by the creative act, enabled him to produce paintings of such intense beauty and apparent simplicity.

When Marion Milner discovered in *A Life of One's Own* that she was terrified of the force of her internal patriarchal God, this cannot all be explained by her introjects of patriarchy but also, as with Matisse and Freud, as an expression of her fear of the creative archetype in all its uncertain raging power. Dionysus, as the embodiment of energy and new life, can also be raving, fearsome, and out of control. However, to be creative the archetype has to be engaged with. For women, disobedience of the patriarchal strictures against creating may be a beginning. Disobeying God, as Eve did, could be understood as part of the powerful side of the feminine archetype that comes into play when one point of view is too rigid. However, the woman has to begin to own some of her aggression in a liberating and creative way. She cannot allow herself to be framed and sidelined for this act, but instead has to take the law into her own hands. Then, for her, the male figure will no longer be needed to be the carrier of her projected creativity and drive.

Marion Woodman sees this stage in the woman's creative journey as a crucial one, which often takes place through an abandonment. "Abandonment means literally 'to be uncalled', symbolically to be without a destiny. If one's destiny has been dictated by a father however, then to be uncalled may be a blessing rather than a curse" (Woodman, 1985, p. 34). If we think of the father in this case as standing in for both the collective and the individual paternal, then through abandonment the woman may have managed to free herself from inhibitions to her creativity. She may have her first experience of feeling liberated, and that she does not owe herself or what she creates to anyone else. However, if she lacks courage then the woman may unconsciously turn her aggression again on herself, become masochistic and, in a spiteful act against her own creative drives, rubbish them. By doing this she would again be aligning herself with the patriarchal world and denying her own innate creativity.

Before she even begins to engage with her creative daimon, a woman's creative desire can be thwarted first and simply by the fact that she is having to fight for a space in the world in terms of work and power. That she also has to fight for a space in the world's mind, where the androcentricity is continuous and almost entirely unconscious, may never be consciously appreciated, but it may be revealed when the fight for a space in the working world suddenly changes. What happens to women when they are given a temporary space in the world of work and power has been well documented around women's roles in the two World Wars. Owing to the need for, and therefore expansion of, women's roles during the wars, there was a resulting disappointment for women when they were expected to return to domesticity when peace came. Both World Wars had appeared to challenge the accepted stereotype of the woman's place as in the home, but when the women were no longer needed for the war effort it became clear that not much had fundamentally changed for women.

Women writers between and after the wars began to document and express their anger that female war work had not changed society's perspective. As creative women they still felt constrained in their creativity by the restricting views of society. However, the anger they experienced also disturbed them. Virginia Woolf, in her seminal essay *A Room of One's Own*, understood about women's rage but saw it as a fundamental bar to true creativity: "She will write in a rage where she should write calmly. She will write foolishly where she should write wisely . . . She is at war with her lot. How could she help but die young, cramped and thwarted" (Woolf, 1945, p.70). Woolf understands that a woman's anger may destroy her art, especially because female anger did not fit into the beliefs of the period that it was unfeminine if expressed. We might surmise that Woolf's own difficulty in accepting her rage was expressed through self-destructive acts in her depression and suicide.

In the 1930s, the French writer Anaïs Nin expressed woman's guilt at writing: "Somehow woman has associated the activity of creating, the creative will, with a masculine concept and has had the fear that this activity was an aggressive act" (Nin, 1975, p. 82). Nin seems to feel that there is no place for a woman to be aggressive, that the emotion belongs solely to men. In her *Journals*, she describes her analysis with the psychoanalyst Otto Rank. "Women, said Rank, when cured of neurosis, enter life. Man enters art . . . The feminine quality is necessary to the male artist", but Rank questioned whether masculinity is equally necessary to the woman artist . . . "'Perhaps', he said, 'you may now discover what you want—to be a woman or an artist'" (Nin, 1973, p. 319). Although Nin does choose to write, it seems that, guided by Rank, she feels that if she is to remain a woman as well as a writer, she has to leave her rebellion outside the door.

When, sixteen years later in 1949, Simone de Beauvoir wrote *The Second Sex*, she described women writers as incapacitated by the amount of energy they had to expend in first gaining their place in the universe: "She is on her best behaviour; she is afraid to disarrange, to investigate, to explode" (de Beauvoir, 1953, p. 666); "Woman exhausts her courage dissipating mirages and she stops in terror at the threshold of reality" (*ibid.*, p. 668). De Beauvoir understands women's fear of disapproval and of disobedience, yet sees this as a fatal flaw that prevents her from creatively forging forward. Her extraordinary ability to do this herself by denying motherhood, aligning herself with Sartre, and harnessing her own rage, made her remarkable in her generation.

These three twentieth-century writers recognized that there is aggression and rage associated with being a woman in a paternalistic society, but they also felt that, unlike men, they had to disengage from these emotions when they surfaced in their creativity, through fear of the impact on themselves or others. As de Beauvoir suggests, the creative act is therefore frequently thwarted to appease this fear. The rage is not seen by these writers as part of the creative act itself. To accept this would mean that rage would have to be explored and expressed as a central *feminine* characteristic.

So how are women expected to view aggression, rage, and rebellion? Can they engage them as tools that they can use for the creative effort? Virginia Woolf and Anaïs Nin seemed to feel that if they owned their anger they would destroy their art. As well as making them feel unfeminine, they perhaps also felt that the patriarchal world would have won; that they would be criticized as mad or unfeminine. Certainly Woolf felt that it was non-productive for a woman writer to plead her cause, but she also understood, like Marion Milner, that for art to flourish there had to be a sense of bisexuality in the creator and that it was "fatal" for a woman writer to write as a woman. Here we might imagine she means it was fatal for a woman to write simply from her accepted femininity, without including her masculine traits.

> And fatal is no figure of speech; for anything written with that conscious bias is doomed to death. It ceases to be fertilized. Brilliant and effective, powerful and masterly, as it may appear for a day or two, it must wither at nightfall; it cannot grow in the minds of others. [Woolf, 1945, p. 102]

Although this was a perceptive understanding of the internal duality that has to happen for a creative piece of work to come into being, Woolf still finds it hard to acknowledge that some of those so-called masculine characteristics of aggression and destruction might also be powerful tools for the female creative enterprise.

The post-Jungian Sue Austin, in her work on women's aggressive fantasies, suggests that if women can acknowledge their destructive desires without acting them out in all their violence and rage, then this can enable them to access their creativity. She also suggests that welcoming these desires is part of refusing to inhabit a handed-down identity where women feel that they are not allowed to have these thoughts. She suggests that it is an essential part of being alive to be in battle with our own identities, to both aim for wholeness and to resist it.

> To lose or abandon the struggle for a unitary identity completely is to move into madness or a form of death: death of the "I" that wrestles with what it is to be me. To become over identified with a unitary identity is to be trapped in a fiction. [Austin, 1999, p. 16]

So it might be that a woman's struggle to explore and define her creative self *has* to be a battleground where images of being an agent of destruction rather than simply the object of destruction are crucial to the creative act.

To experience herself as an agent of destruction would be, for many women, an entirely new frame of reference. A need to keep these possible new identities secret may feel essential but will inhibit a woman's creative self. This idea is explored in the next chapter.

CHAPTER TWO

Using a voice

"Opera is a place where women *cannot* be silent"

(Ross, 1993, p. xxiii)

A s part of my practice as a psychotherapist, I have had the opportunity to work with women who are professional opera and lieder singers. Working with these women, I have found myself in the middle of a dilemma about the mystery of the creative drive: the need for self expression and, at the same time, the apparent necessity for hiding, darkness, and secrecy. It is as if allowing the full-throated expression of ideas, thoughts, and feelings through the singing of them is experienced by these women as forbidden and dangerous. The delicacy and risk of voice-led creative expression brings up specific issues for the singer, who may desire to sing but who may also wish to remain silent. These singers have helped me to understand the tension that is generated between their creative desires and their fears of this creativity. As if to illustrate this tension, they invariably present with psychosomatic voice problems that have resisted medical interventions.

By using an art that expresses itself through constant movement, singers have in their power a force for change, which may move and affect both themselves and an audience. It can be frightening to be in the possession of such a power, and as a result singers frequently try to exert control over and to limit their voices. They may feel that, by singing, they are playing with fire in having the ability to arouse and stir up both themselves and an audience. As a result, they can sometimes express intense feelings of either being burnt or of the fear of being burnt by the profession they have chosen.

Many of the singers whom I have worked with speak of their singing as the most important aspect of their lives and the loss of the capacity to sing as a loss of meaning in life, or, even more strongly, that if they cannot sing it is not worth living. It is as if a loss of the capacity to sing is a loss of a gateway to the unconscious and to the hope and possibility of inhabiting a new identity. However, this gateway is also what is so frightening, for if there is an open and unrestricted flow, then all those feelings and identities which may be seen to be fundamentally unfeminine may be allowed out, and this may feel like a disobedient and unacceptable act.

To make good music is to rouse the gods. When Marsyas took on Apollo in a music contest he not only lost the contest but was flayed alive for daring to presume to match the gods. The retribution meted out for crossing this boundary is shocking in its violence. Singers often speak of feeling "skinless" when they sing, as if they, too, have no protection and will be flayed alive if they dare to let the sound come easily.

The voice problems that singers bring into the therapeutic work symbolize the difficulties they have in allowing themselves a full-throated expression of their innermost feelings, many of which are deeply embedded in the most secret areas of the psyche. Difficulty in producing sound has, in these singers, a protective aspect to it. But these difficulties, such as loss of voice or cracks in the voice, or the loss of the top or the bottom of the voice, can still be deeply traumatic for professional singers. Sometimes they will continue to work despite their problems, resulting in strain on the psyche and voice and permanent anxiety about whether they can rely on themselves. This is more than just performance anxiety. I have not as yet seen a singer for whom anxiety about performing *per se* is the issue.

If all is going well for singers, performing is often a most enjoyable experience. These women, when they come into therapy, often reluctantly admit that they are bringing questions about their psyche and their creative expression, which have been thrown into the open by their struggles with their voice problems.

Most of the singers whom I have seen have already gone through medical assessments and medical procedures and have eventually been told that their voice problems are not physiological, although they may have identifiable physical symptoms such as vocal folds that do not quite meet, or maybe a granuloma in the larynx (a kind of polyp which frequently regrows after surgery to remove it and has the effect of making the singer hoarse or speechless) (Harris, 1998). They may have expended enormous amounts of time, money, and energy on medical consultants, and may have undergone hours of physical therapies or operations to try to resolve their problems. If these efforts have not worked they may feel deeply ashamed that they have not been able to solve their voice problems, and by the time they come into therapy they may be in mourning for what often feels like the loss of their most precious possession.

Psychosomatic symptoms are messages expressed through the body, which can have an elusive and trickster-like quality. Like all psychosomatic symptoms, the symptoms that singers bring are both a defence against progress and an attempt at a resolution. They can, therefore, frequently be intractable. The symptoms always demand attention, but often do not respond to direct understanding or intervention (Kradin, 1997). To understand the symptom may render it obsolete; however, another symptom may soon appear to continue the defensive work. Although consciously the symptom might not be desired, it might also be experienced by the woman as a protective screen behind which her thoughts and feelings can remain secret. Only through therapeutic work with the whole person and a conscious inattention to the voice problems might the symptoms dissolve. Often the first part of the therapeutic work is to encourage the patient's attention away from talking about their symptom. The battle going on may be elsewhere, and, as I shall suggest, the voice problem may also be representing a struggle that is in fact an essential part of female creative expression.

The physical symptoms that singers bring can be lodged in the throat, but more often seem to reside in the upper chest or larynx. The larynx is one of the main organs used to produce sound; it is also at a unique intersection in the body. If the body is pictured as a cross, with the torso intersecting with the arms, it is at the larynx where torso and arms meet and where there is a connection between the external and the internal. It is here that the channel from the emotions and the stomach meets the outside in the form of the arms. The larynx can therefore become the focus for the battle that is being waged—a powerful desire for self-expression that comes up from the stomach and up the trunk and out through the larynx and a similarly powerful rule that this should not happen, which may be experienced as coming from the outside world and from the other, through the connecting hands and arms. This is where the two meet in the physical symptom in the larynx (Shewell, 2002). This conflict may be expressed through pain in the upper chest, neck, shoulders, and arms, sometimes accompanied with difficulty in breathing and palpitations. The voice can be immobilized.

In Kundalini Yoga, *visuddha*, the chakra located in the neck and larynx, is seen as the "seat of speech, and thereby the spiritual centre" (Jung, 1996a, p. 77). I have had several experiences with singers where the emotional force of what they are expressing brings about an extreme physical reaction often in terms of immediate and acute hoarseness, or coughing fits, or extreme loss of vocabulary, or sudden and frightening speech loss.

> When we clothe our knowledge in words, we are in the region of
> *visuddha*, or the throat centre. But as soon as we say something that
> is especially difficult, or that causes us positive or negative feelings,
> we have a throbbing of the heart, and the anahata centre begins to
> be activated. [*ibid.*, p. 63]

These speech crises can be extremely distressing for singers. If some understanding of the violence of the physical reaction (which may happen in the therapeutic session, or even in rehearsal or on stage) and its relationship to the intensity of the emotion or thought and the need to suppress it can be understood, then a channel can begin to be opened up for the unconscious to speak and the secret to be revealed. The secret may not necessarily be about the content of the thoughts or feelings, but more often can be about a sense of embargo about being allowed to express them at all in an active way. This sense of embargo may even extend to speaking *about* the voice. Many of the singers I have worked with have expressed the feeling that their larynx and their voice are sacred to them. This sense of a sacred body part is often connected to feelings of secrecy; that there may be something forbidden or even sacrilegious about discovering more about it.

Every singer brings unique problems, but it seems that, in the area of secrets, there is something that may hold true for many of the female singers I work with. For people who work in other creative or artistic professions, the revealing or the holding on to of secrets is also a central and ongoing issue in the work. This sense of secrecy may be crucial to an artistic work. The work itself may entail revelation or dissembling around a secret kept secret. This would apply to the visual and written arts as well as the performance ones. If there is a lack of secrecy and dissembling, then there is nothing for the reader or audience to work and engage with. Secrets in the arts are essential, powerful, and full of energy. Yet, if kept entirely secret, they can be destructive in their power (if the audience has no access to them then the creative work fails to communicate) or, if inappropriately revealed or the timing is wrong, then they can bring about disaster and a similar lack of communication. Secrets can be magical and mercurial or devious, crushing, and shameful.

A central secret for many women may be about their unexpressed fantasies of aggression or of their desire to slip out of role and inhabit other, less accepted, feminine identities. Although singers spend their working lives borrowing other identities through their acting abilities, this is not the same as self-expression and can often be a defence against self-exploration. A woman who came to see me with voice problems when she was just beginning to make headway in her career began to discover, to her immense surprise, that she had felt neglected and unloved as a child and that she had pinned her hopes on the singing bringing her the self esteem she so deeply craved. She was convinced that her internal world was full of vicious and marauding dogs that would tear her apart if any connection was made with them or if she looked at them more closely. She was afraid of these images and did not wish to own them. However, after a while in the work, she began spontaneously to have images of Weimaranas—beautiful sleek lithe dogs—and she acknowledged her desire to own one of these. As the work progressed, these positive shadow images were allowed more and more space and she began to understand why she had needed the vicious dogs. The vicious dogs were a constant check on her abilities to succeed as a singer and this was needed to prevent her becoming more successful than her father, who was also a musician but who had had enormous difficulties in his career. This realization was one of the secrets that she had had to keep unknown, otherwise there was always the possibility that something might change. Now, in hindsight, I believe that the vicious dogs were also an expression of the energy that she needed to allow herself to step out of role and to become successful in her career. The vicious dogs were an essential part of the dynamic of her creativity. They were representing for her an untapped aggression that she needed to connect into to help her on her creative path and to break from her identification with her father.

When powerful aggressive drives are discovered through the work, women often fear that these secrets about their desires for identity slippage may be revealed, and that the revealing may bring about rejection and a loss of connection and relationship with those closest to them. The patient mentioned above feared that it would come out that she desired to achieve more than her father, and that there was a taboo against this, and that she would be committing a sin by grasping the aggression he had not been able to use for himself. This engagement with aggressive forces, which was necessary for her to move on, would place her, she felt, outside an accepted female identity and this would be a difficult place to inhabit. This was not just a fantasy as it might turn out to be true, since change always disrupts.

These taboos against stepping out of role or inhabiting different identities have the power and force of archetypal fairy stories. These, our most intimate secrets about ourselves and how we believe we should behave and be, are like spells; spells that will send a princess to sleep because she disobeyed a rule; or spells that will render the hero or heroine speechless. Here, secrets and loss of speech are closely connected. The ambivalence about spell breaking can be better understood if it is appreciated as the dangerous archetypal territory that it truly is. Breaking a spell may not necessarily be the right thing to do. Bluebeard's wife disobeyed the rules and opened the doors in the palace. As a result she gained knowledge, but *what* knowledge. From there she could never go back to an earlier, more naïve state. As with Eve, there is always a price to pay for uncovering a secret.

There is often a fear among creative artists who come into therapeutic work that they will lose their muse or their talent. My experience is that this does not happen; rather, I think that if all goes well, the creativity can be developed and broadened, but the fear may be related to this necessity for mystery. In one sense, a singer's voice problems keep the singing safely mysterious and support the unconscious belief that revelation is forbidden. This awareness of doing the forbidden may be especially difficult to appreciate if singing was always the way for the woman to get the attention of the mother or the parents and she was therefore identified in the family as "the singer". On a more unconscious level, the desire to sing may be a way of exploring and getting to know new and liberating emotional states. An enormous conflict can be set up here between the pull to unconscious exploration, which may feel secret and dark and unacceptable, and the desire to shine and impress the parents. To be the golden child appears to offer instant rewards, and the singer may put up enormous defences against the therapeutic work in the hope that the singing can be successful in bypassing the need to go on this journey. This resistance to the work can often happen if an early career has been successful, with no voice difficulties, and it seems that up to this point the desire to shine was enough. A woman in her early thirties came to see me when an early, brilliant career had suddenly crashed when her voice collapsed. The pain and humiliation of this was excruciating for her and she had to make a slow and painful journey towards rediscovering her talent and her self, as if for the first time. This entailed her finding her own voice rather than that of "the singer".

It is an accepted fact between singers that they refer to their voices as "The Voice", as if *it* could achieve fame and identity all on its own as a part object, which does not need to be united with psyche. This does not prevent the singer feeling shame or guilt if "The Voice" fails them, but there does appear to be a culture among singers where to speak of "my voice" would feel too personal, too daring, and therefore too exposing. If it is "The Voice" that expresses feelings, then the woman may feel she can still hide in the shadows. A split can then open up between the body–self axis, and this can become the major psychological battleground. Everything has been invested in the ability of "The Voice" and now this has failed them. This can be experienced as an acute loss of self, as if the voice was The Self itself. The singer may feel that she has no identity and is then faced with discovering other means of expressing herself, and at first this can be excruciatingly painful. "I don't know what I think, I don't even know what I feel", one singer, who had had a long and productive singing career, said to me as she began this process.

Singers ask of themselves a unique kind of creative expression, which relies on externalizing in front of a listening public that which is profoundly internal. Singing has the capacity to access deep layers of the psyche. This is, of course, true of acting and dance and the other performing arts, but through my work with singers I have felt that there is something more acutely exposing about producing sound from within oneself than from other forms of creative physical expression. Sound can be a direct pathway to movement and change, and it may be this that forces many female singers to look at questions of female identity and creative expression.

Sounds can have the power to move us in ways for which we may have no words. The states sounds put us in touch with may be early, preverbal, and even uterine. The mother's heartbeat and the flow of her digestive tract are some of the first sounds experienced by the foetus. As the psychoanalyst Alessandra Piontelli has shown in her extensive work on babies *in utero*, from very early on the foetus responds to the womb, the umbilicus, and its own body in various ways (Piontelli, 1987, 1992). This work has been expanded by the child psychotherapist Suzanne Maiello, in her work on the foetus's experience of the mother's voice (Maiello, 1995). Maiello suggests that the response of the foetus to her mother's voice may be the foetus's first experience of proto-relationship and proposes that the very earliest beginnings of relationship could be entirely based around uterine auditory experiences:

> . . . the hearing capacity of the human foetus is completely developed by the age of four months . . . Low frequency sounds have a

soothing effect on the foetus and slow down its motor activity, whereas sounds of the medium and high frequency range are enlivening and stimulate its motility. The sounds are not only heard by the child, but they seem to leave traces in its memory and constitute a kind of sound-code from which the child's future language will develop. [*ibid.*, p. 26]

Maiello suggests that "sound and music are located ahead of separation", that the foetus experiences sound before it experiences separation from the mother's body (*ibid.*, p. 32). This is a fascinating proposition, that sound is the connection between the foetus *in utero* and the mother, for it underlines the primitive and archetypal layers that singers may connect into.

Language and sound and music may play an important role for the woman who is pregnant in connecting to her foetus. She cannot yet echo her child's sounds, as she will be able to do after the child is born, but, as Maiello suggests, by speaking or singing to her child she could form the basis of a mental container for the child while it is in the womb (*ibid.*, p. 27).

Considering what we do now know about the development of the foetus, it would not, I think, be fantastic for us to understand this proto-relationship between the foetus and the mother, which consists of sound, as replete with archetypal imagery, which exists in a place of pre-separation and pre-language. The adult may be reconnected to this foetal stage of her early development by the use of sound in her adult life, and the resulting experience could be either ecstatic or disturbing, depending on the archetypal images stirred up.

This proto-relationship with sound, then, develops into a relationship with sound and mother after the child is born. At these early stages of development, when the baby is able to make sounds herself, she needs her mother to echo these. At this echolalic stage, before language comes into the picture, the reverberations of sounds between mother and child will become a crucial part of the developing relationship. Sounds made by the baby and the reverberations and reflections of them made by the mother will connect into early and primal bodily experiences for the baby. These experiences may always be associated with certain sounds, although these connections may become more unconscious as the child grows up. If, as Maiello is suggesting, the experience of the mother as *sound* may be the infant's first experience of the Mother archetype, which carries both a terrifying and a creative potential, this would be one way of thinking about why the singers I have seen are both fearful of their talent and the possible loss of it; they experience sound as having enormous power for both ecstasy and destruction.

Another way to think about this early stage of sound, both before and after the child is born, is to see it as the transition phase between the "semiotic" and the "symbolic" order, as defined by the French academic Julia Kristeva. Kristeva's "semiotic" is the baby's experience of the mother's body and the mother's gaze and the mother's sounds before a "symbolic" order takes over with the arrival of language and male order. She describes the "semiotic" as a preverbal energy field that continues to be present unconsciously throughout life. Sound is an important component of that energy field, and keeps the baby connected to the mother.

> Vocal and muscular contractions, spasms of the glottis and motor system all make up for the absence of intrauterine life components. Voice is the vehicle for that call for help, directed at a frustrated memory, in order to insure, first through breath and warmth, the survival of an ever premature human being . . . [Kristeva, 1980, p. 282]

Kristeva names these early experiences of maternal communication as "jouissance". These preverbal experiences of relating to maternal energy are not gender specific and have some similarities to Jung's ideas of androgynous archetypes. There is a capacity here for male–female, feminine–masculine to be undefined, and simultaneously available.

> The semiotic is structurally linked to the mother's body. It is the pre-Oedipal maternal, so it must contain the potential for both genders, as it is *before* symbolic definitions and the understanding of gender as an exclusive binary. Therefore the semiotic is not "the feminine". [Rowland, 2002, p. 120]

Kristeva suggests that once the child moves into the realm of language and the "symbolic" order, the "semiotic" is suppressed and can only be experienced unconsciously as semiotic activity and brought into the symbolic realm through the nature of the creative act. The creative act is therefore inherently subversive through its initial disregard of the symbolic order. Because the semiotic appears before the constraints of the symbolic world appear, the semiotic, as an area of exploration for sound and voice, has the advantage of being *pre* gender definitions, too, a fruitful place for the exploration of the creative feminine prior to the imposition of a patriarchal culture through language.

Music, as an expressive sound experience, is located somewhere between these unconscious worlds and the representational world of word and language. Singers have the power to connect into primitive levels of expression and to touch on undifferentiated emotional states in both themselves and the audience. When a singer sings she may be using language, but is also accessing those layers of expressive sound that come from early and highly emotionally charged areas of her being. Some of these states may arise out of Kristeva's pre-gendered "semiotic", and connect singer and audience together in states of reverie that bypass other forms of communication and affect them in an oceanic way. These states may be very difficult to put into words, suggesting that they are "remembered" as preverbal. This is Oliver Sacks, the neurologist, writing about his confused teenage years:

> . . . the beauty, the love of science, no longer entirely satisfied me, and I hungered now for the human, the personal. It was music especially which brought this hunger out, and assuaged it; music which made me tremble, or want to weep, or howl; music which seemed to penetrate me to the core, to call to my condition—even though I could not say what it was "about", why it affected me the way it did. [Sacks, 2001, p. 276]

To be "penetrated to the core" may be a sense of connection to that terrifying and exciting place that is preverbal, where sound structures, stimulates, and scares, but where language is not part of the experience. This is unknown territory and requires strength and caution and faith for the one initiating the connection. For, if these areas are touched on and connected into, they have the power to affect and change the listener and to make movements in the psyche, movements that may be revolutionary in their creative capacity to bypass the status quo. The stillness in a concert hall after a transforming piece of singing, when for a second or two the individuals in an audience are united in their shared experience, is not similar to any other art form that I know. For seconds or maybe longer, it appears that the internal (the sound from the singer), and the external (the experience in the hall and in the listener) are one. The miracle has happened, there is no separation between internal and external, between self and other, or between ego and self. This experience can feel both transporting and spiritual and can take us on to different planes.

Neil Cheshire suggests that Freud's self-confessed difficulty with music may have been a defence against his lack of control over its effects on him:

> Maybe he came to realize that . . . he could not impose cognitive organization (and hence ego-control) as readily upon his musical experiences as he could upon his aesthetic responses to the verbal and visual arts, and that as a result, his non-verbal musical perceptions were likely to be relatively un-integrated and incoherent. [Cheshire, 1996, p. 1162]

Music does not respond to "cognitive organization"; it exposes the listener to uncontrolled emotional states full of change and movement. Singers have sometimes described to me how strange it can feel when an audience is moved to tears by the sounds they make. For female singers, this experience of controlling an emotional atmosphere in a concert hall may feel exciting, but can also feel alien and worrying. I have had female singers express to me their "guilt" about being able to do this. This is not, as far as I know, a concern of male singers. This worry may be about the sense of doing the unacceptable, of holding the power to engage and move a large body of people. Music has always been known to have the power to carry emotional states of both destruction and healing, because of its ability to stir up and move the emotions. It is in itself the embodiment of movement. Singing necessitates the idea of movement in both the singer and in those who hear her. However, the concept of both moving into and filling out and affecting space is an alien one for women, and runs counter to both historical and cultural ideas that women are the ones who make and contain the space and not the ones to use it. For women to claim space as theirs and to use and move into it would mean embodying new identities, identities that require a sense of feminine agency (Austin, 2005, p. 145). The risk is that these new identities might be brought forth by "being out of control", making a lot of noise, and filling a concert hall with sound. This "forbidden" expression may be greatly desired by female singers but also greatly feared, as it would be transgressing the boundaries of accepted femininity to dominate and grasp space in this way. It is essential, however, for this boundary to be crossed if the singer is going to connect creatively with her audience. To do this she has to grasp her own agency and welcome her capacity to make movement in herself and others. There is an element of positive aggression needed for her to be able to carry this off, an aggression that states, "I have the power to connect with you".

This attempt to achieve a synthesis between the internal and external is, I believe, in various ways what all artists aim for. It is an attempt to confound the difference, the separation between subjective and objective, to create and experience oneness. The artist is driven to recreate this timeless moment as a creative necessity. For many of us this experience of outer and inner matching might be had in a variety of creative ways, or simply by reading a book, or looking at pictures, or taking a walk. For some Jungians these moments might be thought of in a spiritual rather than a creative sense, as an experience of the numinous. For singers, however, this moment has to be produced at exactly the right time in front of an audience and using that gateway to the preverbal, sound. To be able to initiate this oceanic effect in both themselves and an audience, female singers require talent and an understanding of technique, but also, at the same time, an ability to let go and not to be in control or to know what will happen. To reach this place may require the singer to connect into secret territories, to step outside accepted feminine identities and to grasp new ones. You cannot achieve this fine balancing act unless you have both some understanding of yourself, especially your secret self, and also an ability to move into and claim new territories. I would suggest that for female singers it is the fear of moving into these new territories, which the art demands, that brings about many psychosomatic voice problems.

PART II
CREATIVITY AND PROCREATIVITY

CHAPTER THREE

The dilemma of motherhood

"Mothering and non mothering have been such charged concepts for us, precisely because *whichever we did has been turned against us*"

(Rich, 1977, p. 253)

Procreation and motherhood are central creative experiences for women, but they are neither the only ones, nor are they the straightforwardly satisfying experiences that our society would like to believe. In this chapter I look at how the construction of womanhood *as* motherhood denies other avenues of creativity for women. I shall also look at how the idealization of motherhood as always "good" and "nurturing" constrains women's expression of their own true experiences as mothers and makes it more diffi-cult for them to explore their aggressive and ambivalent feelings towards their children which, if acknowledged, could open up other creative possibilities. Finally, I look at whether procreativity and creativity have as many similarities as is sometimes assumed.

A woman's experience of being a mother is as multi-faceted as there are mothers. Feelings expressed by women who are mothers speak of the most intense and tender love through to the deepest and darkest rage, from compassion and altruism through to possessiveness and power. Being a mother impresses itself powerfully on women; it can be fulfilling and devastating in like measure and bring dramatic change to a woman's life. It may be seen by the woman as the most creative of her life's experiences or as a hindrance to her work and creative expression. The state of becoming a mother may be much desired and seen as the central purpose of the woman's life, or it may be feared as an intrusion and interruption to the woman's creativity. Both the longing and the fear are often present at the same time in women who are mothers, and women's subjective experiences convey these dramatic changes and differences. "My children cause me the most exquisite suffering of which I have any experience. It is the suffering of ambivalence; the murderous alternation between bitter resentment and raw-edged nerves, and blissful gratification and tenderness" (Rich, 1977, p. 21).

Our modern collective image of mothers, however, is not only made up of the raw realities of subjective and individual experiences, but is overlaid with layers of cultural expectations and projections. These expectations and projections carry an enormous charge and identity formation of their own, and can make it hard for women to express their multifarious feelings about being individual mothers. Motherhood is now a concept that, as the psychiatrist Ann Dally has suggested, is reinvented with each new age and has social, cultural, and historical meanings that extend far wider than the mere statement of fact (Dally, 1982). This collective image has the effect of constraining our responses to women's identities as mothers, and simultaneously idealizing motherhood and identifying procreation and nurturing as the single most satisfying form of creativity for women.

Mothers are women, and many, or even most women, at one time or another, wish to bear children and become mothers. Procreativity and motherhood are widely accepted and encouraged forms of female creativity. However, the *desire* to become a mother is a complicated and multi-faceted experience, which cannot simply be looked at as "innate" and "natural" and as the inevitable consequence of being a woman. Directly "woman" and "mother" are separated it becomes easier to see the underlying social and cultural dynamics for women once they inhabit the role of *mother*.

The idea that womanliness and motherhood are interchangeable has been questioned and interpreted through the differing lenses of sociology, feminism, gender politics, and psychoanalysis since 1792, when Mary Wollstonecraft wrote *Vindication of the Rights of Woman* (Wollstonecraft, 1975). In this text Wollstonecraft suggested that the supposed intuitive sensitivities of women were not in themselves enough to make women good mothers, and that the woman's mind and her intelligence also had a strong part to play in the mothering role and should therefore be encouraged. Wollstonecraft, who died of puerperal fever after the birth of her second child, lived during a period in which birth and death went hand in hand and women had very little choice as to whether they had children at all or how many they had. As a result child-bearing and rearing frequently dominated their lives. Wollstonecraft's text was therefore revolutionary for its time in suggesting that motherliness and good mothering were not necessarily innate characteristics for all women. Since *Vindication of the Rights of Woman* was published, the debate about mothering has continued in a variety of forms. Women's roles and identities as mothers have been consistently picked apart and examined, specifically during the sexual revolution of the 1960s and 1970s. Yet today, despite the many new possibilities of childcare support and work opportunities that have come about as a result of the growth of feminism and that have helped to open up other identities for women, there is a core belief, which still remains much as it was two hundred years ago. This is the belief, although frequently not acknowledged or admitted, that mothering is *the* fulfilment for all women, and that that is what they are born to do, and that other forms of creative expression for women are therefore less important.

The cultural climate has, of course, changed, in the sense that women can choose careers and opt not to have a family, but the idea that women need to become mothers to be fulfilled remains a belief that is shared by many women and by society at large. This partly unconscious belief appears to have been only marginally affected by the realities and stresses of being a mother in the modern world. It is a belief that inhabits a collective fantasy realm of images, a realm that Rozsika Parker describes as "almost exclusively made up of self-abnegation, unstinting love, intuitive knowledge of nurturance and unalloyed pleasure in children" (Parker, 1995, p. 22). This idealized image of motherhood, in which the mother gives up her own needs and concentrates totally on the child as if this is her singular duty and role in life, remains in the collective imagination despite the liberating effects of possibilities for working mothers and changes in social patterns. This collective image overtakes mothers however much they may believe in their capacities and roles beyond motherhood. When the academic and writer Lorna Sage wrote in her memoir *Bad Blood* about having a child while still at school, and about her fierce determination to continue her education, she found herself surrounded by a mythologizing about babies and motherhood that seemed to have no relation to reality or to the world that she had known and still wished to belong to.

> Certainly it was a lot easier to have a baby than to be delivered of the mythological baggage that went with it. . . . From now on I was making my way against most people's assumptions, I'd have to count my friends and fight back . . . Grandma greeted me as though I'd come back from the Other Side and in a sense I had. [Sage, 2000, p. 265]

The "Other Side", which has suggestions of a parallel universe, is the space where the fantasies around motherhood take hold. Here, women and children are separated off from the living, working world and enter the idealized yet also denigrated world of motherhood. Here women lose their identities as *women* and turn into *mothers*, whose entire duty is to the child and its physical and mental welfare. This ideal mother is a fantasy that has been frequently challenged but has remained largely unchanged in the collective psyche since Rousseau, in his work *Emile*, opened the door to women's guilt in the form of maternal responsibilities in the second half of the eighteenth century (Rousseau, 1902). These responsibilities revolved around the necessity of the mother breast-feeding rather than passing this duty on to another. The woman was to become entirely responsible for the survival and health of her child, the fathers would then naturally play their part, and society would be stable. Responsible nursing mothers would become the linchpin of a virtuous society (Badinter, 1981, p. 168). These ideas reappeared in later periods such as after both the First and Second World Wars, when it was important for the economy that women gave up their wartime jobs and returned to being homemakers. Later in the twentieth century the emphasis on the importance of mothering was again underlined by the birth and growth of psychoanalysis, when the psychological health of children was seen to be the primary responsibility of the mother and theories around the mother–child dyad became central to analytic work.

Nancy Chodorow, the psychoanalyst and feminist, in her groundbreaking *The Reproduction of Mothering*, first published in 1978, explored the idea that mothering was not innate, but was passed on psychologically from mother to daughter through the nature of their primary relationship. The desire for children may feel like a drive or biological urge, but it is itself shaped by the daughter's own unconscious relationship to her own mother and the mother's conscious and unconscious experiences of mothering a daughter. "Women are prepared psychologically for mothering through the developmental situation in which they grow up, and in which women have mothered them" (Chodorow, 1999, p. 39).

Chodorow's central argument was that it was very difficult for women to escape the sense that they *ought* to have babies and mother them because of their own experience as daughters. This experience was formed by a sense of "self-in-relation" born out of the internalizing of a mother–daughter lineage. This meant that female children identify becoming and being a mother as their entry into womanhood, without which they may never feel grown up. Chodorow argued that this mostly made for "good enough" mothering but, at the same time, from her feminist perspective, she advocated shared parenting responsibilities between the couple. In a new introduction to the second edition of *The Reproduction of Mothering*, Chodorow acknowledges "that psychology and politics are not always homologous and that the relative claims of each are not self-evident as we imagine fulfilling lives" (Chodorow, 1999, p. xvii). Here, she reassesses the difficulties of accepting both the uniqueness of the maternal role as well as the necessity of not accepting that this uniqueness constrains women by becoming a construction of womanhood as motherhood. The solution is not simply to share parenting responsibilities. Mothering and motherhood are deeply embedded in women's psyches.

Female patients who are considering having children often express the feeling that they will have failed as women if they do not conceive and give birth, and that anything else they might do with their life will always feel compensatory. This may be partly due to the sense of self-in-relation formed out of the mother–daughter relationship as argued by Chodorow, and also partly due to the social construction that women *are* mothers, which leaves women who wish to have children but are not able to feeling they have failed as women.

This social construction of motherhood has also been supported and underlined by much psychoanalytic theorizing, which has presented good mothering as the subjection of the mother to the needs of the child:

> the ideal mother has no interests of her own . . . For all of us it remains self-evident that the interests of mother and child are identical, and it is the generally acknowledged measure of the goodness or badness of the mother how far she really feels this identity of interests. [Balint, 1939]

Balint, writing in the 1930s, was adding to the construction of motherhood by reflecting a commonly held belief within the early psychoanalytic community that for a mother to mother well there should be no difference between the baby's needs and her own; that it would, in fact, be destructive for the child if there was a discrepancy. Twenty years later in 1956, Winnicott echoed these ideas by suggesting that "primary maternal preoccupation", which he describes as an essential temporary "illness" for the mother, was essential for the well-being of the infant (Winnicott, 1992a, p. 302). Primary maternal preoccupation is still accepted in many psychoanalytic and psychotherapeutic theories as an essential ingredient for healthy psychological growth on the part of the baby, and we know from recent developments in the neurosciences that consistency of emotional attention from an adult is necessary for the growth of certain pathways in the developing brain. Without consistent and empathetic attunement from a carer, the development of the baby's brain is impaired (Gerhardt, 2004). However, ideas of primary maternal preoccupation were developed within a depressed post-war context in which mothers were being encouraged to stay at home for social and political reasons. John Bowlby's theories of attachment and loss, published in the 1950s and 1960s, around the same time as Winnicott was writing, appeared to suggest that to be good mothers women had to remain with their children at all times, otherwise the child would suffer.

> Partial deprivation brings in its train acute anxiety, excessive need for love, powerful feelings of revenge and, arising from these last, guilt and depression . . . Complete deprivation . . . has even more far-reaching effects on character development and may entirely cripple the capacity to make relationships. [Bowlby, 1951]

Bowlby's work has been crucial in our understanding of attachment, but has also encouraged the idea that there was no place for maternal ambivalence or anything but constant attention to the child.

Winnicott went further in suggesting that what was needed for women to be successful mothers was for them to use all their "feminine" characteristics and that these were the essential ones for this task. "When a woman has a strong male identification she finds this part of her mothering function most difficult to achieve, and repressed penis envy leaves but little room for primary maternal preoccupation" (Winnicott, 1992a, p. 302). Although Winnicott is describing what he sees as a necessary absorption with her baby on the mother's part, there is inevitably an implied criticism here: that it would be detrimental to the baby's needs if the mother is as interested in the world outside the nursery as she is in the baby. To suggest that so-called "male" characteristics in a woman prevent her from fulfilling her role as mother is similar to suggesting that men cannot embody the mothering role, which a modern generation of younger men now frequently does. Female identity is neither singular nor consistent, and cannot be constrained by one role. It is

> complex, chaotic and shifting, built around multiple identifications rather than just one or two. A daughter may simultaneously resist and absorb the awareness that she is female, knowing she is a women yet feeling that she is disturbingly male or masculine psychologically. [Maguire, 2004, p. 59]

Both Winnicott and Bowlby understood that consistency of care and sensitivity to a baby's needs were crucial for the development of a balanced adult. They both, within the parameters of their time, saw this as necessarily having to come from the mother. However, this attunement does not have to be gender specific and can be done by any adult who is committed to caring for the baby. Unfortunately, modern society does not offer women a truly free choice as to whether they wish to stay at home with their children or not, by providing consistent and attuned childcare as an appropriate alternative.

The idea of the mother as the person who is both central and essential to the baby's and child's needs became a cornerstone of most psychoanalytic and object relations writing. Since Melanie Klein's work in the first half of the twentieth century, the centrality of the patient's experience as a baby and child with a mother remains the psychoanalytic preoccupation. If the patient in therapy happens also to be a mother, this theoretical preoccupation emphasizes the experience of the patient, as primarily related to her own experience of being a baby, in its reductive and backward-looking emphasis on infantile states as the source of analytic investigation. Although this may be very fruitful, it also inevitably underlines the idea that motherhood can only be spoken of as existing within the mother–child dyad, where the baby is the primary focus and the mother has to dismiss her subjectivity. It can be very hard for women in analysis to feel that their subjective expression of their feelings as a mother, without reference to the baby's experience, is noteworthy and will be valued. It can also be very hard for the female analyst to inhabit other subjectivities apart from the maternal one in relation to her patient. This is what the Jungian analyst, Elena Liotta, calls "the maternalising of the profession" and "an over development of the maternal and self-renouncing elements in the therapeutic stance, which contribute to a pushing aside of the analyst's individuality as dangerous to the holding environment that the maternal emphasis insists on" (Liotta, 1997, p. 317). This "maternalising of the profession" can be a trap for female analysts and therapists by emulating a way of relating in which they may already be embedded without questioning whether this is appropriate.

The image of the mother–child dyad as a self-contained oneness dominated by the needs of the child is not simply the result of society's needs and projections and the development of psychoanalytic theories, but is also underpinned by centuries of images of mother and child. Images painted in the Italian Renaissance by Leonardo da Vinci or Botticelli of the Virgin and Child (Figure 1), or in twentieth century artistic expression such as the sculptures of mother and child by Henry Moore, where mother and child are carved from one block of stone, are profound images that have the power to move us and to resonate with our desire for completeness and for fusion. Although this idyllic image of motherhood is not one that contemporary artists are now particularly interested in addressing, surrounded as they are by the reality of modern motherhood

Figure 1. Botticelli's "The Virgin and the Child", 1480. Courtesy of the Museo Poldi Pozzoli, Milan.

with all its tensions and pressures and ambiguities, this idealized image of mother and baby in a fused state is still very present in our culture.

> Often, I was still reading in bed while Erica and Matt slept together beside me, his head on her breast as she held him. Even while she slept, she was aware of him and would wake to his smallest squeak. Sometimes, I would put down my book and look at the two of them in the light of my reading lamp. I now think I was lucky that I wasn't young. I knew what I might not have known earlier—that my happiness had come. [Hustvedt, 2003, p.38]

In Siri Hustvedt's novel *What I Loved*, the arrival of Matt is experienced by both the protagonist and his wife as a numinous event. I quote from this remarkable novel because of the way the writer manages to convey the extraordinary in the ordinary, which we can all experience at the birth of a child. Birth is one of the few places where we still allow the sacred to enter our modern existence.

However, this luminosity of birth and babies for the collective and for society as a whole means that mothers carry layers of idealization and projection that it is almost impossible for them to live up to. Idealizing a person or an idea means that there is no space for anything negative to come in. There is literally no possibility of any view except one of perfection. This, coupled with the fantasy that mothering is "natural" for women, creates an unquestioned presumption that women *are* mothers rather than the fact that mothers are women. I do not mean to suggest that this unique oneness with a baby is not experienced by mothers, or by fathers for that matter, but rather that there is a tendency for it to become *the* collective image of motherhood and then, because of its power, it can, in effect, marginalize other forms of creative expression for women. Behind this idealization of motherhood lie feelings of envy and denigration on the part of men and hate and rage on the part of women, which, if acknowledged, might help this ideal to become more of a creative reality.

Jung's ideas help us to deconstruct somewhat this self-perpetuating, closed image. Jung saw the psyche as forward looking; that who or what the person might become was even more important than where she had been. This enables the rigidity of the totality of the mother's responsibility to be lessened somewhat. The baby or child has creative capacities to relate both to its mother and other care-givers and also to its own archetypal images of the mother, which may be stirred up and formed by early experiences of its mother's body. Jung understands the baby as being able to relate to its mother on more than just a personal level.

> She was our first experience of an outside and at the same time an inside: from that interior world there emerged an image, apparently a reflection of the external mother-image, yet older more original, and more imperishable than this—a mother who changed back into a Kore, into an eternally youthful figure. [Jung, 1956, p. 324]

The archetypal mother, who is experienced by the child, has not only the capacity for nurturing and care but also embodies a prospective pressure towards the future and individuation. This archetypal capacity, which the mother carries, has nothing to do with a rigid, gendered idea of mothering, but rather a capacity for movement and change and therefore destruction as well as nurturing. The capacity of the archetype to hold these two poles not only enables the child to struggle with love and hate, or, in Melanie Klein's terms, both the good and the bad breast, but also, I would suggest, it offers the mother herself an opportunity to deconstruct the image of primary maternal preoccupation and allow her own subjectivity to enter her experience of motherhood and to experience it as valid for both herself and the child.

Both the psychoanalytic and the religious image of maternal preoccupation reflect an absorption in a pre-oedipal state of grace on behalf of the baby and also of the patient looking back. An archetypal mother, however, also holds the possibility for the baby and the adult of an energy, which pushes towards the future and towards change. This mother holds within her the destruction of the dyad, the necessity of separation, and the possibility of hate as well as love.

> The archetypal mother partakes of all the multiple plurality and numinous resonances of archetypal images. This means that the mother can stand for the divine, spirituality, the body and, crucially the *future* direction of the person's psyche as well as the past. [Rowland, 2002, p. 115]

If a woman who is a mother has the capacity to engage the baby's psyche in future possibilities as well as representing the containing present, then her role as mother can also embrace the idea that there are other identities that she can inhabit for herself. A patient who was weaning her child struggled painfully with her feelings that she both mourned the loss of breast-feeding but also felt a driving urge to be rid of the baby and have space and time for herself. This space was for her own creative expression, which was entirely separate from her identity as a mother. She felt that if she allowed herself to fulfil this need, she would be seen as, and experience herself as, a bad mother—that her desire to separate and follow her own creative path as well as mothering her child was inherently wrong, that her creativity was not acceptable unless it was in relation to her child. Elena Liotta argues that it is women's inherent natural capacities for nurture that stand in the way of other creative endeavours:

> In view of such natural capacities, any psychological and symbolic development of creativity in a woman is bound to be more laborious and complex than the parallel process in a man. It will mean abandoning natural advantages to cultivate something other that feels unnatural. [Liotta, 1997, p. 320]

This sense of wanting something that feels unnatural encourages feelings of guilt, shame, and rage, which can overpower women during their mothering years.

Young-Eisendrath recalls similar ambivalent feelings during the early years with her children:

> Perhaps the most poignant (as I reflect back on my darkest pre-feminist hours) were the dreadful times I spent in remorse and shame, afraid of my enraged and sometimes murderous feelings toward my delightful and beautiful babies. These feelings would overwhelm me at times, especially at night when I would drag myself from bedroom to bedroom attempting to soothe and nurture and contain what was troubling my children. [Young-Eisendrath, 2004, p. 89]

It is this ambivalence to the mothering role that is central to both the child's and the woman's well-being, as Rozsika Parker has so cogently argued in her book *Torn in Two*. Rather than seeing the woman's murderous feelings towards her child as "unfeminine" and "bad", Parker suggests that we should look at maternal ambivalence as a source of energy and change.

> A relationship perceived as constructed out of empathy, identification and "at one-ness" must involve a denial of the reality of hatred and overlooks the contribution the negotiation of mother–child hatred makes to the personality development of mother and child. [Parker, 1995, p. 160]

One of the positive aspects of this "negotiation of mother–child hatred" would be an encouragement for women to differentiate themselves from *mother* so that their identity is not simply reduced to the maternal function. Acknowledgment of hatred enables an essential separation to happen between mother and child, which otherwise constrains them both. It also then opens up the possibility for loving feelings to be expressed. If neither is constrained by the other they are free to love, "mothers hate their children because they are expected to love only them and not engender and love anything else" (*ibid.*, p. 250). Parker argues that the difficulties of mother–daughter separations demand that we consider maternal ambivalence and aggression as positive aspects of motherhood.

We might think of these mostly suppressed and rejected feelings as the energy that is needed to break open Chodorow's "self in relation", which she sees as the inevitable generational experience of being mothered and mothering for women. This could be an energy that separates the self from relation and allows mothers to let their daughters go, as well as enabling daughters to leave their mothers. This may be experienced as a destructive force but, if accepted as a positive and creative force, maternal ambivalence has the capacity to bring women's subjective experiences as mothers into the forefront of our collective images of motherhood and to help women break free from the uncreative images of idealization and denigration. If women's ambivalence about their roles as mothers was brought into the main body of psychoanalytic thinking as a positive aspect for both the mother and child, rather than interpreted as a mother fighting against her "natural" role, psychoanalysis would have finally left behind the social and cultural mores of its founding fathers.

It may be helpful to look at the actual experiences of pregnant women to realize how often images of destruction and death do appear alongside those of love and nurturing. Most women who have been pregnant have had disturbing dreams or fantasies about what the baby may do to them or what they may have done to the baby. Sometimes these are of the baby dying, or of how the mother may have damaged the baby by her life style or destructive thoughts. Sometimes it is the baby who is the destructive one, the parasite who will engulf the mother or eat her up. Identification can move between being the mother and then the baby inside, sometimes it seems there is a battle being waged and opposites are often in conflict. In an extensive study by Abt, Bosh, and MacKrell (2000) of the dreams of pregnant women, powerful, destructive, and creative images are examined, which the authors see as inherent to the nature of procreation. These dreams of the collective and archetypal elements inherent in procreation represent the maternal in the broadest possible spectrum of feelings—from destructive and Kali-like to loving and nurturing. The editors see the dreams as essential to the working through required by women who are pregnant of the opposites of life and death, power and weakness, hate and love. These opposites are stirred up by the psyche when presented with pregnancy as an elemental creative force.

The psyches of pregnant women are bombarded with archetypal expressions and structures, which suggest that the process they are in is going to turn out to be more multi-faceted than any idealized image of a united mother–child dyad might suggest. Kali is an appropriate goddess to call upon here, for she is the Hindu goddess of creation *and* destruction. Her rage can destroy but it can also create. The pregnant woman needs this multi-faceted creativity, which involves allowing the destructive or deathly images that come to her in dreams and fantasies to be acknowledged as an essential part of the procreative process.

> I am fighting with a prehistoric being, perhaps a dinosaur. All his entrails are out in the fight, but something remains latent as a seed for its subsequent development. However I have the feeling, at least for this time, the battle was won. I am playing with little figures of clay. There is a little girl of clay, and she comes into life like a human being. [Abt, Bosch, & MacKrell, 2000, p. 171]

In this dream there is a fight with a cold-blooded destructive power, which the dreamer wins, at least for this time and with this baby.

Motherhood presents women with stark life and death issues, both in the realities of the potential physical dangers inherent in pregnancy and birth and in the archetypal images stirred up and activated by the process of creating a life.

> You have only to listen to mothers to see that the biological experiences involved in pregnancy and mothering, and unconscious as well as conscious fantasies about these, are deeply central to women's sense of self and one of the central meanings for women of motherhood. [Chodorow, 1999, p. xiii]

The biological experience is directly related to the mother's fantasies and the physicality of the body experience relates directly to a sense of self. It is the effect of pregnancy and birth on the woman's body and the unconscious fantasies associated with this that can encourage the woman to enter motherhood appreciating and trusting what she might see as her negative as well as her positive feelings towards the child.

Psychotherapists, as well as poets and writers, are fond of using words such as birth and pregnancy to describe other forms of creative process. The forthcoming book or painting becomes a "baby". The writer or painter is "pregnant" with their work. In her book *Dying and Creating*, Rosemary Gordon suggests that procreation is like other forms of creativity in that they all require an ability to be open to receive the unknown and for there to be a mother who receives and a father who gives (Gordon, 2000, p. 134). As I have argued elsewhere, this meeting of male and female elements may have symbolic resonances in creativity and procreativity, both for those who can and for those who cannot conceive (Miller, 2003). However, this language may also become a limiting factor for women in attempting to express their subjective experiences of motherhood and creativity, for it does not speak truly for the maternal.

The inherited and accepted language of motherhood does not adequately reflect the violent and destructive aspects of the imagery of procreation and does not, therefore, when used as a metaphor, adequately reflect the creative experience either. Women who become mothers have a struggle to express the whole area of motherhood in subjective terms and to speak of multiple female identities. Many of these identities may not be experienced as a fluid interplay of male and female elements or as contained as some of the literature suggests.

In her extensive writing on the maternal realm and language, Julia Kristeva suggests that language, because it is based on what she calls a paternal signifier, marginalizes the experience of the maternal and the feminine. Language can therefore only speak *about* the maternal rather than *for it* (Kristeva, 1980). However, this gap can be bridged: "Kristeva sees the artist, poet or painter, due to the very nature of the creative act, as having the potential to bridge the split between the maternal and paternal signification" (Adams, 2003, p. 60).

The creative act may therefore be fundamentally different from the experience of procreativity, in that it has the ability, when working well, to bypass the language that speaks *about* and become a language that speaks *for* subjective experiences. This may be an important difference between procreativity and creativity that gets lost if we refer too easily to the "births" of books or poems or paintings. The book or the painting speaks for the woman in a completely different way than the baby does. In a healthy society women should feel that they can experience both.

CHAPTER FOUR

The problem of infertility

"The crying of a baby is not a sound I can block out; it is as if the child puts a hook into the flesh above my navel and reels me in. The touch of small children makes my breasts ache. 'No children?' a woman once said to me. 'Never mind, you've done your books'"

(Mantel, 2003, p. 25)

For women who are unable to have children, the complicated relationship to creativity becomes darker and more difficult to unravel than for women who are able to conceive and give birth. However, as with women who do become mothers, the areas of conflict, ambivalence, and deathliness can become richly creative if they can be accessed. In this chapter I explore what the experience of not being able to conceive when you wish to is like for women, and how devastating this may be to a woman's sense of her creative potential. I also look at how this blocking of procreativity for women can be turned into a tool for a deeper exploration of the creative self. By looking at the subjective experiences of women who wish to but cannot conceive, I attempt to highlight how the experience of being infertile can either become a dead end or be turned into a new creative understanding.

As I suggested in the previous chapter, for women who are pregnant, the multiple changes in both physical and psychological arenas as the foetus develops may be experienced as dangerous and can appear as such in dreams. In the dreams of women who cannot conceive, destructive battles and dead liminal creatures can also appear as symbols of an internal battleground. It seems that the area of destruction and creation is symbolized in similar ways in both pregnant and infertile women.

Through working with women who are struggling with infertility issues and with the prospect of not becoming mothers, I have been able to understand more about how creative avenues can get swallowed up, or simply hidden by the intense desire for procreativity. Without the capacity to conceive and to give birth, a woman may feel cut off from all her creative capacities and experience herself as living only within the deathly end of the creative archetype. The woman who longs for a child yet remains childless is brought up against issues of death and mortality within herself and her own body in a different way than for a pregnant woman.

The relationship of the birth process to transience, death, and destruction as well as to joy is, as I suggested in the previous chapter, something women who become mothers come up against in a powerful way. Yet we all struggle with these poles as part of the experience of being creative human beings. A beginning cannot be meaningful without an end, and without a beginning it may feel as if there is only an end. There is a tension between birth and death as they are inextricably linked together and inform each other. If, in the experience of infertility, this tension is severed and there is no concrete birth, then body and psyche may be experienced as unconnected. In this void-like place, the idea of conception may be identified as either having miraculous qualities or it may be obsessively pursued through medical interventions maybe at great physical and mental cost to the woman or couple involved.

Conception is one of those facts of our humanity that still holds mysteries for us. It inhabits a place between psyche and soma, somewhere between the angels and the corporeal body. It is an issue both grounded in the physical world and yet rich with symbolic meanings; an area inhabited by gods and angels and yet made concrete by the conception and birth of human babies. Our responses to births and deaths may be one of the few ways we still allow ourselves to acknowledge that we are connected to a spiritual life. A patient told me how her partner had been completely surprised by overwhelming feelings when his brother had his first child. It was as if he had been out of touch with this area of himself before that and was now aware of his own procreative desire and maybe also, as a result, his mortality, his fate as a human being.

Many patients come into therapy because they feel empty inside or uncreative, and fear that there is nothing there or that what is there is destructive. For patients who are infertile, these feelings can be compounded. Some of my female patients have been unable to conceive children. Some have decided not to reproduce. Many have allowed the decision to be made for them by the passing of time. For those who cannot conceive there is a difference between those for whom a medical reason is found and those who have "unexplained infertility". Primary unexplained infertility, where no cause can be found for the inability to conceive, has special issues relating to it, which bring up profound experiences of loss of both identity and the capacity for creativity of any kind. This painful psychic state can appear to leave them stranded in a place that is neither of the living nor the dead, literally in limbo. Conceiving or miscarrying, or suffering from blocked tubes, or ovarian failure, or any of the many medically recognized reasons for infertility, presents the patient with reasons for, and realities of, loss. There is a failure to conceive, and this can be painful to accept or mourn, but there is a loss, which can be thought about and pictured in bodily terms. For those who have unexplained infertility, there is no loss but rather a void. No embryos, however young, no damage, however guilt-ridden, can be focused on, there is simply a space into which a child cannot or will not come, and about which it seems that nothing can be known. This lack may become for the woman an image of all aspects of her creativity. If the concrete child cannot be made, symbolic children also feel entirely out of reach and the idea of them may be experienced as a poor substitute.

In his *Visions* seminars, Jung refers to this internal struggle for a woman who is unable to get pregnant as "a special kind of hell. For a woman there is no longer any way out; if she cannot have children she falls into hellfire because all her creativeness turns back to herself, she begins to eat herself" (Jung, 1997, p. 794). Jung's rather dismissive comments about the creative capacities of childless women have to be taken within the context of his time, but they also highlight his difficulties in fully appreciating women's similarities to men as creative beings, as well as their differences. However, Jung does understand the powerful internal destruction experienced by infertile women, which is frequently a source of deep guilt and can result in destructive self-attack. Although we now know that issues of infertility are shared between women and men, the power of the "barren" woman who is thrown out of her marriage and rejected by society still echoes powerfully in our modern world.

> Potentially deprived of reproductive choice, we are thrown back into the instinctual feminine world—the archetypal realm of the Mothers—where, for millennia, infertility has been perceived as failure, or worse yet, a curse, often accompanied by family isolation or ostracism. [Finiello Zervas, 2003, p. 191]

As many modern feminist writers have also noticed, for the infertile woman, something more than the possibility of a baby has been removed: "It seems that once you find yourself involuntarily childless, all other identifying marks are washed away. Of course such transformations are not unusual; they are the hallmark of socially stigmatized conditions" (Pfeffer, 1987, p. 82). There is more at stake here than an inability to make children. As Pfeffer argues, this may well include a sense of social stigmatization, but I consider that the lack of "identifying" marks goes further than this. A woman who has no explanation for her infertility can experience herself as not only socially but spiritually and psychically severely disabled; and, as Finiello Zervas suggests above, there is an archetypal realm of isolation and curse underlying it all. These are powerful levels of psychic disturbance to deal with and, as a result, the infertile woman may be unable to function on many levels.

During the past two decades, medicine has embraced the infertile in a major effort to "cure" this state. It is now more than a quarter of a century since the first test-tube baby was born. Since then, assisted reproductive technology has grown dramatically. Every year there is a new breakthrough in terms of assisting those who are unable to procreate and everyone now knows of someone who has had IVF. These extraordinary medical advances may appear to provide a concrete answer to healing the childless state, which is now seen by modern society as unnecessary. Changing expectations of procreative choice have played a part in dramatically affecting the expansion and proliferation of these medical interventions. It is now a widely held belief that all women should have a baby if they want one, regardless of age or fertility issues. There is a concomitant acceptance that infertility is a medical problem with a medical solution. As a result, many women and childless couples have been successfully helped to have families. However, there is a powerful shadow side to these medical interventions. The treatments themselves can cause illness and can have long-term medical effects on both mother and child (Finiello Zervas, 2003). These interventions may also prevent the woman who continues to have unsuccessful treatment from engaging with her own inner creative strengths, as I have argued elsewhere. "The medicalisation of procreativity can create its own obsessional pathology and prevent an exploration of loss and destruction which may be crucial to creative recovery and renewal" (Haynes & Miller, 2003, p. 5).

To live within this medically attuned age not only opens up new solutions to making babies but it can also become a defence against other forms of creative awareness and understanding. The medical consultant and forms of assisted reproduction can be seen as the saviours, to be pursued at all costs. The fertile and creative spirit then appears to reside with them and not with the couple. The hundreds of photographs of babies emblazoned on the walls of infertility consultants' offices appear as signs of the fertility of the consultant, or his magical powers, rather than that of the woman and her partner.

Most infertile couples who seek treatment are not successful in producing a child. Yet if the desire for a child becomes an obsession, the couple may feel that hope would be lost for ever if they were to stop looking for a medical solution. This may be regardless of the threat posed to meanings and relationship by repeated technological interventions. Many couples break up while undergoing treatment and the need to have sex to order frequently results in the loss of any erotic relationship.

> With IVF came a gradual decay of hope. We weren't in control of our destinies. It's a course of action I would recommend people to

think very, very, very hard about. Because it's a high-stake game and the odds are that you will lose, and continue to lose. [Gerrard, 2001, p. 20]

Despite these dangers, any suggestion that there might be other ways of looking at this deathly state to help warm it into life, apart from a birth, can be experienced as an additional unbearable wound, much like a prisoner might experience if told that her release was not the primary issue and not what she should be thinking about. Studies of infertile couples who attend infertility clinics are now beginning to acknowledge that protracted medical interventions can become anti-therapeutic and anti-healing. Acknowledging an infertile state as permanent can help a couple to adjust (Koropatnick, Daniluk, & Pattinson, 1993; Moller & Fallstom, 1991).

For some infertile women, for whom reproductive technologies have not turned out to be the answer, an acceptance of their failure to conceive may not release them but may keep them imprisoned in a state of permanent failure. In this prison there appears to be no escape, no space for psyche and soma to talk to each other, and no possibility of other creations. Those who suffer from unexplained infertility may then experience a ghostly form of loss and death that appears to be especially difficult to work with or through, as there is no subject to mourn or death to be known about. Ways of dealing with other losses and usual coping mechanisms for grief seem inadequate and irrelevant. This lack, rather than loss, may have differing psychological effects. There may be difficulty engaging with the mourning process, but there may also be an accentuation of an emptiness that is already felt to be there. Or the effect may be to reactivate old losses. As a result, the woman may feel she is presented with an existential difficulty around a loss of identity and self.

Frances had come into therapy in her forties because of pain about her inability to conceive over a long period, going back to her mid-twenties. She longed to be released from a frozen state where a baby would not come and yet she could not move forward into her life. No medical reason had been found for her infertility, which left her with a void. "It would be a miracle if I got pregnant now. I don't know why I can't conceive and yet I have no hope because all I have is this nothingness." In using the word "miracle", it was as if Frances could only see a solution to her problem as happening outside herself. How was it possible to engage with a dynamic internal world when, in a physical way through her body, she appeared to be uncreative?

She spoke of how, if she had been pregnant once, even if only for a few weeks, this feeling would have been different. She would have known that she was fertile even if the pregnancy never came to term and she never gave birth to a child. Becoming pregnant to prove fertility and a capacity to create can be experienced as a separate issue from actually giving birth to a child. In Eva Pattis Zoja's interesting study of abortion, she looks at women who abort again and again rather than use contraception and sees these repeated conceptions without a birth as attempts to initiate a birth of self through the constant re-experiencing of fertility (Pattis Zoja, 1997, p. 31). The choice that some women make to abort a foetus may sometimes be an attempt to step outside a recognized feminine identity of belonging to the world of mothers, where ambivalent feelings may have to be denied.

Pregnancy has always been a visible statement and proof of fertility and virility for both women and men. When a woman is unable to make this happen, the lack of a concrete expression of her procreativity can feel like an attack on her capacity to trust in any of her creative acts. It may confirm a sense of being empty inside and having nothing to draw on. "I could never have babies. I felt empty—well I was empty, wasn't I?" (Gerrard, 2001, p. 21) Or it may confirm a fear of being full of unseen destructive forces, which are not available to be known about except through their results.

For a woman who has unexplained infertility, an experience of an active duality of both creative and destructive forces can appear to be absent. She may experience her womb as neither a container nor a coffin, simply an empty space. This, as I suggested in the previous chapter, may be partly to do with the language, which speaks *about* and not *for* women's experience, and the way in which this language speaks of women *as* mothers. This language will simply reflect an emptiness back to the infertile woman.

Psychoanalytic imagery of women's bodies as containers for the penis or the unborn child—as houses, vases or enclosed spaces—reinforces the link between female eroticism and maternity. Can we find new ways of theorizing sexuality which allow women—whether or not they are mothers—to have their own autonomous identities, their own sexual lives? [Maguire, 2004, p. 68]

So, for the infertile woman there is a double problem: she has only the language, which speaks *about* her infertility in terms of a lack. This void not only separates the woman from her creativity but also from her destructiveness. It appears that, unlike a woman who can become pregnant, she can only speculate about the forces within but cannot *know* about them. A connection may be helpfully reactivated if she does become pregnant. The psychoanalyst Joan Raphael-Leff sees pregnancy as a catalyst in this regard:

> Pregnancy, like all transitional phases, reawakens earlier unresolved conflicts and anxieties. The archaic clash between her inner imagined life-giving and death-dealing forces is now relocated in the arena of birth, a test, culminating in proof of whether she is destructive or creative. [Raphael-Leff, 1985, p. 16]

Some infertile women connect their own lack of mothering to their present inability to become a mother. If the mother was a negative figure and remains an internally negative one, then to become like her by having a child may be strongly resisted in the unconscious. This resistance and ambivalence is, of course, around for all mothers and potential mothers, as I suggested in the previous chapter. The mother's realization that she may have murderous feelings towards her own child can be very shocking as well as liberating (Parker, 1995).

Whether an unconscious ambivalence can be so strong as to deny conception was one of the questions that Frances had to struggle with and which we could only speculate about in the work. There may be many contraceptive scenarios that the unconscious may play out; an area that both Freudian and Jungian analysts have speculated about. The unconscious fantasy of being able to have a one-parent conception may reduce fertility (Mariotti, 1997). Or a difficult intrapsychic relationship between the woman and her own mother may add to difficulties in conceiving (Pines, 1993). These difficulties may be played out in the relationship with the therapist, which becomes the stage where meaning can be made from the patient's experience of nothingness.

For Frances, the reality of her infertility felt so concrete to her that she defended against symbolic interpretations. Early on in her therapy, imagining other ways of making "babies" seemed to be very painful. It was as if anything that she might create could only be seen as a poor substitute for a real baby. For us to make connections in the process of the work required her not only to trust me and her journey, but to allow an intimacy between us and expression of feelings that felt extremely dangerous to her. As the work progressed, it was the expression of her rage and aggression that brought us closer together.

Not to be able to conceive is to experience an extreme limitation that can suppress feelings of both aliveness and death. There is no sign of a birth, but nor is there any sign of a death. A patient who was questioning her own single state and lack of babies reported, with amazement, how a friend of hers, who was in her late forties, and who had so far not been able to conceive, had a near-fatal car crash and became pregnant immediately afterwards. She was not sure how these two events were related, but felt somehow that they were, that the brush with death had enabled her friend to conceive. She had come close enough to her own death, looked it in the face, and also her own capacity for destruction, to be able to give birth.

For a woman who is experiencing unexplained infertility to get in touch with destructive thoughts, or dreams, or fantasies, can be difficult. Many of my women patients will do anything to avoid expressing these feelings to me. They cannot experience a difference between the thought and the act, and they seem to fear their loss of identity and acceptance as women. Struggling with the difference between omnipotent destructive fantasies and the desire to live them as a reality is a crucial part of becoming an individual and refusing a handed-down identity (Austin, 1999). We all long to tear down, attack, release our rage, and have murderous thoughts, yet for women to acknowledge these thoughts threatens them with a loss of their identity as a woman. The thoughts may therefore be expressed unconsciously through repeated abortions or difficulties in conceiving. This is not to say that all women who have unexplained infertility may have unresolved issues around these destructive aspects. We do not yet know nearly enough about all the factors involved in conception. However, with studies now beginning on couples prior to IVF, it does seem that the more these couples are able to be aware of their unconscious ambivalence to pregnancy and parenthood, the more successful the IVF treatment is (Christie & Morgan, 2003).

For many years Frances was unable to acknowledge any ambivalence that she might have about being a mother. When there appears to be no choice there is no place for ambivalence. Nor could she express her anger or rage about her infertility, only her unresolved grief. She clung tenaciously to the belief that her anger would only make things worse for herself and those close to her, and that it would be destructive of any creativity she might have. Because of their continuing strong desire to have a family, she and her partner went through the lengthy process of becoming accepted as adoptive parents. When a seven-year-old-girl was eventually matched with them, Frances realized at the very last minute that she could not adopt the child, although she knew this was her last chance to be a parent. Although there were clear concerns about whether this child would be able to settle, this was not the overwhelming reason for the decision. Frances was incontrovertibly faced with her own ambivalence about being a mother. "I can't do this because I fear that I will be lost, that what I need will be forgotten about. I am terribly ashamed that when I am faced with becoming a mother it is not the most important thing in my life. Maybe if I'd had my own child, I would have had no choice, but here, now, with this little girl I can't do it." The shame and guilt associated with making this choice for herself, rather than for another, seemed to herald a turning point in the work. The crisis that was experienced as a result of making a decision seemed to open up for Frances the possibility of naming and talking about her ambivalence about becoming a mother and enabled her to acknowledge her capacity to say no to a child.

During the lengthy adoptive process, which consumed most of her waking thoughts for many months, she often questioned why she never dreamt of this future child who was to be so important to her. During this period no representations of this child came into the therapeutic work. In an interesting parallel, Pattis Zoja compares the dreams of two women who are considering abortion. The one who decides to abort never dreams of her child and the one who decides to keep her baby dreams frequently of "my baby". Pattis Zoja suggests that both the absence and the presence of an image have an effect on the final decision of the two women, that one had unconsciously decided to embody the child and one had not (Pattis Zoja, 1997, p. 79). This relationship to image has been highlighted since ultrasound has enabled a mother to see pictures of the child in her womb. The daughter of a friend, who had decided to abort her second child because of external difficulties in her life at the time, was unable to do this after she had seen the foetus on the ultrasound screen.

Images stirred up by archetypes are full of creative energy, and these psychic images, together with those around us in our society and culture, can become rich mixtures for creative thought. In modern society, the ultrasound picture can have the power to connect the pregnant woman with the idea of being a mother. Once the image is there, whether through dream or ultrasound, there is something to respond to on an imaginary or emotional level.

For Frances, once the decision not to adopt had been made, the little girl appeared frequently in her dreams, as if, now the ambivalence had been acknowledged, she could be made flesh. This was a painful realization, but it also enabled the beginning of a mourning process to happen, for now there was someone to mourn. Frances's need to go through the lengthy and painful adoption procedures eventually enabled her to move on. This was achieved through what she experienced as a destructive act on her part. If the possibility of adoption had been given up before the arrival of the child, this would not have had the initiatory meaning for her that she needed it to have. For her, the rejected child was her sacrifice, as with a woman who aborts a baby, a painful choice that she knew she would live with for the rest of her life. This loss empowered her, as she realized that she did have a choice and that she had *chosen* to reject this child. "I could have been a parent if I had wanted but I decided not to be. That is very different to feeling that the choice has been denied to me. Now I know that I shall never be a parent. Something has come to an end." It is as if to release themselves from the prison of infertility women need to do that which will mean risking their last vestiges of female identity, which in many ways they already feel they have lost. They have to give up their sense of powerlessness and contact their destructive side, and rediscover their capacity to act.

Marion Woodman, who sees part of the woman's psychological growth as separating from her mother, suggests that violence and destruction may play a part in this:

> If she can hold the tension until she finds herself, then her baby if she has one, will not have to carry what she has fearfully avoided. An abortion can be the threshold that forces a woman to seek her own identity, in which case the baby becomes the sacrifice through which the woman brings herself to birth. [Woodman, 1985, p. 119]

The life and work of the Mexican artist Frida Kahlo gives us an insight into how acknowledging destructive forces can be closely linked to creative output. In 1925, Kahlo was in a bad car crash, which almost killed her and prevented her from studying medicine. In 1932, after marrying the artist Diego Rivera, Kahlo suffered a miscarriage, after which she was unable to bear children. It was from this point that Kahlo began to explore a new identity as a painter. She had originally attempted to abort this child, and she was fully aware of her own ambivalence towards motherhood. Nevertheless, the miscarriage was deeply disturbing to her, and, although it was unusual for the time, she requested to see the foetus and to be given illustrated medical books so that she could under-stand what had happened to her body. Images from these books appear throughout her work as a painter.

Soon after coming out of hospital, she made a series of drawings and paintings relating to the miscarriage. In an extraordinary litho-graph entitled "Frida and the Miscarriage" (Dexter & Barson, 2005, p. 36), she explores the beginnings of her birth as an artist and its relationship to her body. Frida stands naked and upright. The picture is divided down the middle and centrally through her body. From her eyes drop large tears. On the left of the picture is the foetus, with its umbilicus wound round her leg and above it; copied from scientific illustrations are cells dividing. On the right of the picture there is another form of creativity. Drops of blood from Frida's uterus fertilize the soil. Plants which partly resemble the human foetus grow from the soil. A third arm from Frida's left shoulder holds a painter's palette. Above this a weeping moon appears, a symbol of fertility weeping for the infertile woman.

In her lithograph, Kahlo rejects the standard cosmology in which Woman is subordinate to Man. Instead she meticulously reconfigures an alternative scene in which the male partner—and the sun that is his symbol—are conspicuously absent. Kahlo images herself as an autonomous creative being, reborn as an artist. [Ankori, 2005, p. 38]

In this picture Kahlo is acknowledging that her body has failed her as a mother, but she sees herself participating in a fertile and creative way in both nature and art. Kahlo is often quoted as saying that "two accidents" shaped her life. The first was the crash, which almost killed her, and the second "was Diego" (*ibid*., p. 32). As the art critic Ankori suggests, the "accident" of Diego Rivera certainly resulted in a tumultuous relationship that shaped her life, but it was only after she stopped being a wife and trying to be a mother that she grew into a painter (*ibid*., p. 34). For Kahlo, it is as if the shock of her own ambivalence and the resulting loss of the baby catapulted her into expressing her creativity in an autonomous form through painting. Painting then became the form through which she discovered and reflected often on her body and herself. In "My Birth" (1932) (Figure 2), the first painting she made after her symbolic rebirth as an artist, she defies all conventions and paints her head coming out of her mother's uterus directly towards the viewer as if in a medical illustration. A picture of the Madonna hangs over the head of the bed, but this could not be further from a Christian nativity scene. The mother's face is covered, as if to deny her importance. Although Kahlo may be reflecting on her own difficult relationship with her mother, she also seems to be painting the birth of the self. Although this idea has reverberations in some modern interpretations of the Virgin Birth as a symbol of the birth of self for modern women, Kahlo's painting does not hide the violence of birth behind images of mother–child purity. In "My Birth" there is uterine blood and pain, which accentuates the impurity and visceral nature of coming into being.

Throughout her life, Kahlo's paintings continued to be predominately self-reflective. Her many self portraits appropriate the self as subject, presenting art historians of today with an endless potential for exploration of her identities in political, social, and personal contexts. Her creativity uses as its subject the self, but this self was

Figure 2. "My Birth", by Frida Kahlo, 1932 (oil on copper). Courtesy of Banco de Mexico and Instituto Nacional de Bellas Artes. Private Collection, Madonna. Photo: Jorge Contreras Chacel.

brought into being through the pain and sacrifice of giving up the expected identities of wife and mother. Kahlo used her two "accidents" to enable her to access her creativity. It may be something about this capacity to use the destructive and violent aspects of having a woman's body that appeals to so many women who love her work. Kahlo dares to speak of the violent shadow sides of women's bodies and their mothering capacities in a way that resonates with her primarily female audience. Whatever we may think of Frida Kahlo's work, her self images are constantly reinvented and reinterpreted as images full of creativity and imagination. There is an energy in her painting, where she shows she is not afraid of the visceral qualities of the female body or of representing *woman* as antithetical to *wife* and *mother*. Her still-life painting is some of her most beautiful and sexually charged work. In "The Bride Frightened at Seeing Life" (Dexter & Barson, 2005, p. 169), painted in 1943, a diminutive doll-like bride peers over the edge of luscious tropical fruit. Kahlo leaves us in no doubt that the erotic and creative potential of married life, for this young woman, is a daunting and potentially dangerous prospect. In "Fruits of the Earth" (cover), painted in 1938, the visceral quality of the fruiting bodies has a powerful erotic charge but there is also a whiff of rotting nature in the painting. For Kahlo, being female means dissolution, death, and destruction, and the necessity of engaging with a creative daimon to survive. There are in her work frequent references to the oppressive gender roles in Mexican society, and she shows us how she struggles to be independent of these proscribed roles through her intense creativity. It is through her painting that she speaks consistently *for* women's creative struggles.

There is a marked difference between those infertile women who long for children and are never able to move into other areas of creativity and those women who are able in some ways to do this, as Kahlo did triumphantly. Neither may ever, as the self-help books suggest, come to terms with their childlessness, but they may learn to cope with it (Bryan & Higgins, 1995). The losses and grief continue into middle age and old age as the lack of children evolves into the lack of grandchildren and the pains return in different ways and in different forms.

However, through the pain of isolation and loss, the infertile woman may be in a unique position to make important shadow feelings conscious. This knowledge may be crucial in enabling her to access her creativity in other ways. As Marion Woodman suggests, "The biological purpose of life at the unconscious level is to reproduce itself, the conscious purpose is not simply to reproduce or perpetuate but to *know*" (Woodman, 1985, p. 119).

PART III

CREATIVITY AND PSYCHOTHERAPY

CHAPTER FIVE

History, gender, and relating

"The end of analysis coincides with the acceptance of femininity ... the termination of analysis ... coincides with the termination of misogyny, when we take Eve back into Adam's body, when we are no longer decided about what is masculine and what feminine, what inferior, what superior, what exterior, what interior"

(Hillman, 1992, p. 292)

T he psychoanalytic world, in its beginnings in the early 1900s, was dominated by men. Both Freud and Jung developed their new theories in the context of a history and a culture where women were expected to play out specific "female" roles. Despite the difficulties of being accepted into the new world of psychoanalysis, there were a few women who made an enduring mark in those early years. Melanie Klein followed in the wake of Freud and made a significant impact on the psychoanalytic community, spawning a theoretical school of her own. Toni Wolff, Marie-Louise Von Franz, and others took up Jung's work and developed it further. But it was only in the second half of the twentieth century that increasing numbers of women came into the psychoanalytic field. Many of these women therapists have opened up thinking about masculine and feminine and about roles and gender (Maguire, 2004; Ulanov, 2001; Woodman, 1992; Young-Eisendrath, 2004). These psychoanalysts and psychotherapists have attempted to influence a profession that was male dominated, but, more crucially, whose clinical theories were born from and built upon an androcentric perspective of the world. This perspective, which sees everything in the psychological arena from a male perspective and bases its theories on that viewpoint, has become one of the core problematic issues for the psychoanalytic community in the twenty-first century. As the Jungian and archetypal psychologist James Hillman suggests in the epigraph, the ongoing split and separation of masculine and feminine is at the heart of why we all need psychoanalysis in the first place. In this challenging statement Hillman does not see this split as a side issue, but as central to the health and creativity of all of us, both men and women.

In this chapter I look at the beginnings of psychoanalysis, with an emphasis on Jung and the women who worked with him, to highlight issues of gender and sexuality that are still unresolved areas today. I trace the beginnings of Jungian theory around the feminine, and the dilemmas women faced as analysts and patients in this emerging profession. I do this by looking at the work of two of Jung's early female collaborators, Toni Wolff and Sabina Spielrein, and at one of his most important but forgotten patients, Christiana Morgan.

In the early 1900s, female creativity was thought of as embodying one pole of a limiting archetype of the feminine, which was structured around relationship and mothering. Women were seen either as fulfilling a nurturing/mothering role or, occasionally, as a companion and intellectual mate to the man. This image of feminine power idealized women's capacities as relational beings, either as mothers or companions, and therefore inevitably also brought forth the shadow side of misogyny and attacks against this power

Jung's views about men and women, masculine and feminine, and anima and animus have been a source of great debate and confusion for analysts and scholars alike, as he is not consistent in his writing and does not always differentiate between the sex of the individual and their psychological sense of their gender. This means that he may use "feminine" when he is actually meaning "woman", or "masculine" in a derogatory sense if applied to a woman. This would simply be typical of the chauvinistic attitude of the times; however, he also developed a theory of archetypes that is one of the most liberating and revolutionary ideas to come out of psychoanalysis. His theory of archetypes states that all archetypes are androgynous and plural, so, for instance, we all possess both masculine and feminine characteristics. This opens up possibilities for a discussion of gender politics and is the main reason why feminists, analysts, and academics continue to develop and work with his ideas. As the academic Susan Rowland outlines in her *Jung. A Feminist Revision*: "Androgynous archetypes are multiple and have a compensatory role to ego experiences. The mind can never be of one fixed gender and archetypes will *work with* and produce *contrasting notions* of the femininity and masculinity witnessed in material culture" (Rowland, 2002, p. 40).

It should, therefore, follow that the two types of mental functioning that Jung proposes, Eros, with its qualities of feeling and relating, and Logos with its qualities of intellect and rationality, are available to both men and women. However, as some post Jungian writers suggest (Samuels, Shorter, & Plaut, 1986; Young-Eisendrath, 2004) this does not translate into Jung's more misogynistic view that: "In women on the other hand, Eros is an expression of their true nature, while their Logos is often only a regrettable accident" (Jung, 1982, p. 171). When Jung is aware that his own thoughts and comments about the feminine do not fit in with his theories of androgynous archetypes, he writes that these conflations he makes are the result of the projections of his own anima (the archetype of the feminine in his unconscious) on to a woman. So the woman is often written about by Jung as the receptacle for his anima projections rather than from her own subjective experience.

The positive aspects of Jung's work on gender helped to place the feminine in a central position in psychological thought, and he appreciated that the repression and wounding of the feminine were sources of ongoing cultural sickness. However, like many of his contemporaries, Jung also displaced *women* from this central position and in this way took a part in that repression and wounding. He used his own personal ideas and experiences of his anima and projected these on to women, and by so doing he removed women from a central position in culture, history, and thought. As Susan Rowlands interestingly suggests, it was Jung's desire to become a medium himself that led to his displacement of the feminine on to his own internal voice or anima. In doing this, "Jungian psychology contains a gender politics in a drive to displace the feminine into the position of 'other' (anima) to the masculine psyche" (Rowland, 2002, p. 19).

Sabina Spielrein and Toni Wolff, who both learnt to be analysts under Jung's influence, struggled with the gender and relational aspects of the new theories coming out of Switzerland. The work of these two women highlights two very different ways of trying to make this new world of male generated ideas and language speak equally for the female. Both women are studied and referred to today, although Spielrein was all but forgotten until a book about her and her relationship with Jung and Freud was published in 1980 (Oucharenko, 1999, p. 369). They also, in the context of their times, both challenged this androcentrism by bringing their own experiencing into the theoretical discussion. By doing so they attempted to carve out a place for women's psychological life that was not filtered through a male viewpoint. Toni Wolff did this by highlighting the plurality and diversity of the relational aspects of women's roles to men, whereas Sabina Spielrein attempted to break open the narrow construct that understood sexual relating as a positive creative drive by looking at the necessity of destructive forces in creativity. Toni Wolff remained a collaborator with Jung and held a unique position in his life, while Sabina Spielrein was sidelined by Jung and, as a result, moved to Vienna to join Freud before returning to Russia, where she worked as a psychoanalyst and eventually died at the hands of the Nazis.

Toni Wolff, who was Jung's lover and then his confidante and collaborator for over thirty years, began her relationship with Jung by having an analysis with him and becoming his student. She was a highly intelligent woman, and known to be an extraordinarily gifted analyst who enabled patients to access deep areas of their unconscious. Wolff did not publish very much, maybe partly, as Tessa Adams suggests, because of Jung's concern that her intellect might be used to challenge his position (Adams, 2003, p. 22). However, in the area of clinical work with patients she was allowed to shine, and was highly thought of by her female analysands, who felt she was prepared to go into places in the unconscious that Jung may have been more wary about with his female patients:

> When Dr Jung came back from New Mexico, I had no wish to go back to him for regular sessions. I trusted Toni Wolff and knew that she gave me the kind of support, which was needed for the unfolding of the unconscious process. [*ibid.*, p. 21]

The qualities that Wolff had of nurture, support, and constancy in the face of the dark demons in the unconscious perfectly fitted Jung's view of the *femme inspiratrice*, whom he needed for himself to help him face his own unconscious processes. Wolff embraced her role as *inspiratrice* and companion to Jung, and helped him to contain and analyse the unconscious fantasies that threatened to overwhelm him at various stages of his life. The relationship became intimate on both a sexual and psychological level. Thereafter, Emma, Jung's wife, had to put up with their long and sustained collaborative efforts. Prior to Toni Wolff's appearance, Emma had been the one to fulfil the role of Jung's collaborator. Presumably in an effort to justify the change in his own mind, she was now compartmentalized by Jung into the role of wife and mother, although she continued to do her own analytic work (Bair, 2004).

Tessa Adams suggests that Jung's anima projections on to the two most important women in his life influenced the work that they did.

> For instance, we can interpret Emma Jung's focus on the male-soul image, through her study of the anima, as the means by which she grappled with the vicissitudes of the male psyche in a bid to mitigate the confusion of the unfaithfulness which Jung brought into their relationship. Similarly, Wolff's exploration of the complexity of the feminine, in her *Structural Forms of the Feminine Psyche* (1956) can be interpreted as the process by which she validated her submission to the weight of Jung's paternal dominance. [Adams, 2003, p. 9]

Both women were assigned roles that suited Jung's needs perfectly, but this limiting of the female to eros and relating curbed the women's creative expression to a single field, mother *or* intellectual companion. This reflected his own inclination to split the image of the feminine in two.

It is in her most important paper, "Structural forms of the feminine psyche", that Wolff attempts to carve out a niche for herself
within the constraints of her relationship with Jung. In this work
she draws initially on Jung's work on psychological types, but
develops it to produce a broader map of the feminine psyche. She
begins from Jung's premise that, "the soul, i.e. the psyche, is the
feminine principle, the principle of relatedness, while logos
abstracts and generalizes the individual" (Wolff, 1956, p. 2). It is
from an acceptance of this principle of relatedness for women and
rationality for men that she suggests that there are four types of
relatedness that women fit into: the Mother, the Hetaira (who is a
companion to the male), the Amazon (who is independent), and the
medium or medial woman (who is the guide and support in helping the man access his unconscious).

Wolff's four types open up more possibilities for women, but
still identify women in terms of their roles in life rather than their
experiential existence. Wolff states that "all four structural forms are
inherent to every woman, although there will be one form which
predominates" (*ibid.*, p. 9). Each of these forms expresses itself
through relationship to the male, except for the Amazon: "To be the
wife of a distinguished man means nothing to her; she strives to
win the laurels herself" (*ibid.*, p. 7). The negative side of the Amazon
form is expressed as one of "misusing human relationships as a
means of 'business' or for the sake of her career" (*ibid.*, p. 8). It is
the Amazon form which suggests possibilities of an identity separate from the one that takes relating as its central premise; however,
this was perhaps an ideal rather than a reality for Wolff, and it is
the Hetaira form that is generally considered to reflect her own
view of herself in relation to Jung. "She will convey to him the sense
of a personal value quite apart from collective values, for her own
development demands of her to experience and realize an individual relationship in all its nuances and depths" (*ibid.*, p. 6).

Wolff's ideas did not challenge the female/eros/relational
aspects of Jung's ideas, and nor did she grasp the possible openings
for female experiencing that exist within his ideas of the androgynous archetypes. However, in the context of her privileged position
within the Jung household, and as a single woman without a
doctor's qualification, it would have been damaging for her to put
herself up as a challenge to his authority, as Jung's support was

essential to her. She would also have been aware of the difficulties that had arisen between Jung and another of his articulate and intelligent female collaborators, Sabina Spielrein.

Sabina Spielrein was Jung's first psychoanalytic patient and was analysed by him in the Burgholzli mental hospital in Zurich. She was also the first of his female patients to become a colleague after her analysis. For a short, intense period she became for Jung a highly charged erotic object. Whether the erotic relationship was consummated remains a subject of debate. However Jung brought it to an end, resulting in intense pain for her. Spielrein was in love with Jung, but eventually moved away from his circle to join Freud in Vienna, where she worked with him for a while before returning to Russia, where she became well established as a psychoanalyst. As in his later relationship with Wolff, Spielrein initially represented a *femme inspiratrice* for Jung, a female figure who could help him connect to his imaginative unconscious. After Jung ended the affair, Spielrein rejected this role for herself in favour of a wider personal creativity and developed her work within a Freudian framework.

In 1912, while she was still involved with Jung but was beginning an analysis with Freud in Vienna, Spielrein wrote a seminal paper, "Destruction as the cause of coming into being", which she presented to the Vienna society just as the rift between Jung and Freud was coming to a crisis (Spielrein, 1994). It predates much of the work done by Freud on the death instinct, and uniquely suggests a relationship between sexuality and destruction. Both Jung and Freud appeared unaware of the importance of this paper, Jung initially misreading it and then upsetting Spielrein by suggesting there were "uncanny similarities" to his own work, and Freud dismissing it as too personal: "her destructive drive is not much to my liking, because I believe it is personally conditioned. She appears abnormally ambivalent" (Kerr, 1994, p. 403). Freud eventually acknowledged her ideas on destruction at a much later date, when he was working on his own death instinct theories.

In her paper, Spielrein proposes that it is inevitable that destructive forces play a part in the sexual drive and the nature of the creative act.

> Self-preservation is a "static" drive because it must protect the existing individual from foreign influences; preservation of the

species is a "dynamic" drive that strives for change, the "resurrection" of the individual in a new form. No change can take place without destruction of the former condition. [Spielrein, 1994, p. 174]

There is an energy in her paper that goes to the heart of her struggle to find an independent creative self; a creative self that is not proscribed by an emerging science that is inherently patriarchal. Her work is revolutionary for its time, as she touches on the creative possibilities of her own capacity for destruction within sexuality and how this holds the possibility of being able to engage with her own creativity. Spielrein applies her theory to both men and women. But for a woman, a break needs to happen in her capacity and expectation of relating as fundamental to her nature if she is to create. This is what Spielrein did by stepping outside the accepted rules of what constituted an understanding of the female gender.

As the Russian academic, Victor Oucharenko suggests, Spielrein uses her own experience of her relationship with Jung to work out her theory of sexuality, but, unlike Freud's initial critical view, which places her work only in the personal, Oucharenko sees her work as "an original, significant and forward-looking concept, created at the very limits of the psychoanalytic tradition and touching upon the most fundamental problems of the psychoanalytic problems of man" (Oucharenko, 1999, p. 360). Her idea turned on its head the psychoanalytic theory of eros prevalent at the time. She had used her own female experiencing to understand a fundamental truth about creativity for both women and men: that destruction in some form was essential. To understand that transformation cannot happen without dissolution or destruction of the previous way of being is fundamental to ideas of transformational healing. "For Spielrein, the ability to dissolve and transform became the central unconscious mode of psychological processing and simultaneously acknowledged the symbolic value of controlled aggression (destructive symbolism)" (McCormick, 1994, p. 188). This idea of dissolution is also implicit in alchemical writings, which were taken up later by Jung as a model for the process of individuation.

Spielrein also indirectly challenged the idea that connection is inevitably a given for femaleness. For women, the "destructive symbolism" mentioned by Mc Cormick above, might entail a shedding of role. In Sue Austin's extensive exploration of women's aggressive fantasies, she quotes one of her contributors as describing the necessary rejection of relationship and responsibility that happens when she paints:

> Isla: "When I paint I feel omnipotent. I think it's the closest I'll ever come to the 'God' or a higher being. Or maybe it's what men feel like. It's a thrill and even more so because I rush at it (daring it to last) and still it lasts. I'm sure it's the power that men must feel: I've created so I can move forward." [Austin, 2005, p. 123]

Spielrein attempted to break out of the gender politics of the day by rupturing the idea of relating as a fixed given for women. Wolff embraced the idea of relating and attempted to find a secure space for herself within her own structures of what she saw as innate female characteristics. It was Jung's desire for a *femme inspiratrice* that supported and made possible the long collaborative relationship between him and Wolff. This was where Wolff made meaning for herself and discovered that she had a certain power, but only in relation to the great man. Wolff's ability to serve Jung's unconscious in this way encouraged a body of Jungian work that took as read the essentialist nature of women's relating to men, rather than the more revolutionary and liberating ideas that Spielrein expressed around the necessity for destructive fantasies. It is only relatively recently that Spielrein has been rediscovered, and books and plays have been written about her suggesting that she played a crucial and pivotal role in the early history of psychoanalysis (Hampton, 2002; Kerr, 1994; Marton, 2002). This earlier dismissal of ideas that challenged an androcentric perspective is an example of how analytic theory can so easily close down, rather than open up, discussion of the female experience and, at the same time, maintain the status quo.

Christiana Morgan was a highly gifted and beautiful woman who sought an analysis with Jung after her lover, Harry Murray, had approached him for advice as to whether he should leave his wife for Christiana. She brought some extraordinary and powerful material of the female experience to Jung, who in the end was unable to contain it and to allow her experience to drive the analysis. Morgan responded intuitively to Jung's method of exploration and trustingly used her analysis with him to go into very deep areas of her psyche. "She also appealed to Jung as a woman, for in her dark reverberative beauty and her deep connection with the unconscious, she resembled his own anima image" (Douglas, 1993, p. 148).

Morgan was struggling with comprehending her own earthiness as well as the spiritual aspect of her sexuality. As Claire Douglas suggests, this struggle paralleled Jung's own, and the work could have been very creative for both of them. However, because she was a woman, Jung was blinded to her possibilities (ibid., p. 150). Instead of supporting her attempt to go deeply into an area of chthonic feminine understanding, he suggested that she live her life in a similar way to Toni Wolff, as a supporter to her lover. Morgan was confused about this advice about her lover, Harry Murray, and wrote in her journal, "I feel him to be clutching and tearing at me for something—as though he would tear the secret of his own love out of me—and at times with him I feel absolutely exhausted and drained dry" (ibid., p. 152).

Jung's advice was especially unfortunate for Morgan, as she had discovered that she had an extraordinary ability to produce visions, which she was able to work with and put down on paper. Jung was thrilled with her visions, but was unable to respond in an appropriately analytic way. He understood the potency of how the visions connected her back to a dynamic feminine, but, rather than encouraging this journey, he wanted to appropriate them for himself.

> Neither Jung the man nor nineteenth-century theory expected this sort of unconsciousness in a woman. Men faced with this feminine power tend to flee, or to combat it by seizing it for themselves, trying to surmount it by lovemaking or rape. [ibid., p.164]

Claire Douglas argues that Christiana's central and important vision of a naked goddess, on fire and with snakes writhing from her head, could have become a powerful focus for the analysis, but Jung enviously compared her snakes with bigger and better ones of his own, and the analysis disintegrated because of his inability to allow her to claim this aspect of her powerful femininity (ibid., p. 165). He seemed unable to imagine her psyche as self organizing, and he confused her need for a trusted man to support her on her internal journey with his own idea of what she needed. "You are like Brunnhilde. You have never been broken in. There ought to come to you a Siegfried who would break through your ring of fire—who would make you into a woman" (*ibid.*, p. 166). It is not difficult to see that Jung's own Siegfried fantasies may have been behind this desire to invade and possess.

Christiana Morgan was certainly ahead of her time in that her visions showed dark aspects of the feminine archetype, active and dangerous ones to do with Lilith and Kali, but they needed to be loved and nurtured if they were to help her individuate. Claire Douglas, using extensive letters and notes from the Morgan family archives, argues that this was a tragedy for Christiana, who was never able to live up to her extraordinary abilities. She published very little, a couple of papers with Henry Murray in *Genetic Psychology Monographs* and *Archives of Neurology and Psychiatry* (Morgan & Murray, 1935, 1945) and a paper of her own on the thematic apperception test (Morgan, 1938). Jung, meanwhile, used her three vision notebooks as the basis for his series of Visions Seminars, putting himself and his own methods into her visions and creating a powerful series of seminars that are still highly thought of today (Jung, 1997). The visions remain, but they were appropriated and were not allowed to serve the woman to whom they belonged. Christiana Morgan's experience of the chthonic feminine could have advanced Jungian thought and pointed a way to a psychological understanding of women from a powerful individual subjective experience, which would have benefited both men and women.

The situation for female practitioners and female patients has changed dramatically over the past century. Women's own experience does now form the basis for much therapeutic intervention and support. But some of those original theories, which categorized women as relational beings over a hundred years ago, are as difficult to address now as they were then. The psychoanalytic and psychotherapeutic worlds have grown up around the idea that relationship and connection with another person are essential for therapeutic work to happen. The therapeutic encounter cannot be transforming unless there is a basis for relationship between the two people involved. This model takes as its starting point that we are inherently relational and dependent beings, and that it is through relationship and an acceptance of our interdependence that exploration can happen and healing may be found.

Developmental and object relations theories are primarily based on the early mother–child relationship. Although new work has been done in the last decade on father–child, and relationships between siblings, the mother–child dyad remains the centre of the relational matrix of modern Freudian and Jungian work, and also all those other therapies that have grown out of psychoanalysis. Winnicott's "good enough mother", Klein's "good breast/bad breast", Jung's archetypal "earth mother", are all examples of the mother–child dyad in differing forms. As I mentioned in a previous chapter, the theoretical approach of the mother–child dyad has implications for the understanding of the subjective experiences of women as *mothers*.

Development of these ideas of analyst as mother–container has resulted in a tightening of theories, which now, unlike in Jung's day, emphasize the necessity of the analyst putting her individuality aside and taking a self-abnegating stance. Many object relations trainings adhere strictly to this model, and see any comments from the analyst that are not to do with the patient or the transference situation as bad practice. Although these boundaries may often be essential for good practice, this theoretical approach can easily become a sacrificial and masochistic way of life for the therapist. Liotta links the problem of creativity for women practitioners to exactly this self-denying nature of the profession. She says,

> [the psychotherapist] faces a paradox which makes psychotherapy almost impossible as a profession: to give in to the other's needs means to give oneself up; however, giving oneself up, one is no longer creative enough truly to give to others. [Liotta, 1997, p. 317]

It is this theorizing of putting oneself second and providing space for the other that may exacerbate the difficulty of internal exploration of creativity for women psychotherapists. I am, here, distinguishing between male and female psychotherapists and how they may respond, not because I believe that men are less able to be empathetic or nurturing, but rather because of the effect I believe the legitimization of these characteristics has on a woman's ability to access her creativity. Putting aside her own needs so as to be able to hear those of her patients may already be a fundamental part of her experienced identity. It is, therefore, more difficult for her to mount a challenge here as to whether that identity is innate, constructed, or chosen, or whether it could be subject to change. For male therapists, putting aside one's own needs for the good of the work does not necessarily mean detaching from one's own creative expression, as the male landscape of nurturing and empathy does not come weighed down with the same historical, sociological, and archetypal resonances that fill women's psychic space. For men to be mothering does not mean that they carry the social construction that mothering inevitably means womanhood at the expense of other womanly identities, as I have suggested.

The theorizing of these mother–child images, whether they are enacted by men or women, are part of what Young-Eisendrath calls "psychological determinism"; a tendency of psychology to accept without question men's experience of women as if they were actually images of women. It is this tendency to see everything from a male perspective that is now deeply embedded in many theories of psychotherapy.

> Object relations theory and many of the infant–mother theories of development are replete with men's accounts of the mother–child dyad, even including the experience of the mother! In order to differentiate the female person, in her own subjectivity, from the male person's "object of desire and dread", we must begin with women themselves. Great trouble and sadness can arise for female people in importing male meanings and imaginings—men's fear and fantasies about mothers and "powerful" women—into the central holding place of female psychology. [Young-Eisendrath, 2004, p. 94]

Jung, Freud, and other early disciples of psychoanalysis were often caught up in countertransference enactments with their female patients without understanding what was happening when their female patients fell in love with them. Jung's abuses of Toni Wolff , Sabiena Spielrein, and Christiana Morgan were not, I suggest, an unconscious reaction to self-abnegation on his part, but rather because he appreciated what these women had to offer and wanted some of it for himself. The result was a blurring of the boundaries between patient and lover and, as a result, as in all abuse, the women, instead of being released, felt tied to him.

Unlike Freud, Jung did not stipulate an analytical technique, and many Jungian trainings now spend as much time on object relations or Kleinian technique as they do on Jung's writings. However, this lack of a technique is a very positive and important aspect of Jung's work. He believed that the therapeutic relationship came out of the relationship between two people. For him, it was the meeting of the unconscious imaginings and fantasies of both people in the encounter that was the creative work. This capacity for unconscious influence and meeting on both sides is a central experience of Jungian work, and one with powerful creative potential for both parties. However, this way of working holds the possibility of women patients experiencing movement and change in their ways of relating and in their experiences of gender identities, which can be very powerful. Like Isla, who paints and feels like a man, they can slip into other ways of being. This can be true for therapists as well as patients, if they are interested in this way of working and do not feel constrained by theory. However, because it can be so powerful, and both fascinating and seductive, there is a shadow side to this way of working, which can result in various forms of abuse of the patient. This is partly why clinical theory has become so prevalent, although in its effort to contain and protect the analyst it has fallen into the same shadow.

There are many ways in which an analyst can abuse a patient. I am, here, interested in the ways in which both male and female analysts can pass on abuses of the feminine that may be endemic to the theories they follow. The abuse may be a reaction to the constraint put upon the therapist by an over-zealous theory of self-abnegation. I do not intend to suggest that theories of psychic life and treatment are not fundamental tools for therapeutic work, but they can all too easily become rigorous analytic superego demands or an internalized patriarchal insistence on one way of thinking which stifles creative work. "The repressed Self rebels and must get back its energies from somewhere, thus feeding itself within the analytical relationship that has starved it" (Liotta, 1997, p. 319). Alternatively, the abuse may come from an envy of multiple feminine subjectivities that may be released through a creative analysis.

As Gabbard and Lester clearly delineate in their book on boundary violations in psychoanalysis, those first boundary transgressions in both Freudian and Jungian schools shaped the birth of the new profession and gave it a legacy that has been difficult to change (Gabbard & Lester, 1995, p. 84). Partly as a result of dealing with patients' powerful transferences, and because of the fear that boundaries are easily broken, theories that have developed out of the early psychoanalytic movement have formed themselves around a benign image of feminine power, that of the mother. This has left both the creative and shadow side of the feminine in the unconscious of the profession, which is a very dangerous place for it to be. In the next chapter I look at how fear of this unconscious feminine is passed on between generations within training institutes, and how this can stifle creativity for those who wish to train as therapists.

CHAPTER SIX

Patriarchy and hate in training institutes

"Our problem is not so much to foster creativity but to try not to inhibit the creativity naturally stimulated by the nature of the work"

(Kernberg, 1996)

During the process of training to be an analyst or psycho-therapist, many things conspire to prevent creativity in candidates. This squashing of creativity is to do with the history of the profession, the theories pertaining to it, and the fears generated by the nature of the work. In this chapter I examine how all these issues come together in the training process and form a patriarchal belief system that is expressed as aggression towards the feminine.

The psychoanalytic profession is unique in the way it is struc-tured, in that therapists and analysts become professional members of the body that trained them and then remain members of the same organization as long as they are practising. This means that they may never leave their training institute or the people who analysed them, taught them, and supervised them. This is highly problematic, as it is very difficult to grow beyond those who have taught you and to develop your own thinking if you cannot leave the nest. To remain with the parental figures means struggling with irresolvable issues of power, and eventually encourages a masochistic withdrawal and submission to the status quo. Many training institutes kill off the energy and enthusiasm of their new members simply by keeping senior members in power for far too long. To opt out and leave the organization means to lose much of what has been worked so hard for in terms of status and a sense of belonging, and registration as a therapist may be dependent on remaining a member. To be accepted into another analytic group may involve being re-examined all over again as being fit to belong.

Training to be an analyst or therapist is an extraordinarily demanding process, both emotionally and financially, which may go on for five, six, or seven years, involving an ongoing personal analysis, work with training patients, supervision of these patients, and regular weekly seminars. Unless you have private means it is necessary to have an income from a job at the same time, and as the years go on it becomes more expensive as patients and therefore supervision increases and training fees may go up. To both begin and then sustain this process, you either have to be deluded or have enormous faith in the work, or maybe even both. To be prepared to put so much investment into the training means that it is also very difficult to give it up or train somewhere else. Although some candidates do leave during trainings, many more of them may deal with their ambivalent and resentful feelings by trying to ignore them so that they can stick with their choice.

Candidates are often disturbed to discover that they are re-enacting childhood patterns of compliance during their training, and sometimes long after it has been completed. Although a certain amount of regression can be expected in any educational situation, some analysts have noted how analytic trainings seem to have difficulty in distinguishing between levels of candidates' knowledge of psychotherapy (which may not be extensive) and their experience of life (which may be very rich), and as a result are more likely to treat them like children rather than adults (Reeder, 2004, p. 163). The sense of having committed oneself and "made one's bed", combined with an awareness of having to remain with the parental figures after qualifying, is not conducive to an atmosphere of creative questioning and debate both while training and after-wards. Lip service is paid to the idea that newly qualified analysts will no longer have to face the same child–parent issues when they become colleagues. In fact, the sensitivity of post analytic relation-ships and the difficulty of dealing with unexpressed feelings between analysts, supervisors, and ex-analysands means that this can result in an impasse where, in a small organization, it becomes almost impossible to further collegiate relationships in any way. These problems do not encourage a culture of creative, ongoing dialogue between candidates and members. Communication between members themselves may be overlaid with an atmosphere of paranoia and fear of change, which they have brought with them from their own years as candidates.

This sealed space within which candidates become analysts is unique in professional trainings and creates therapists who fear contamination from ideas prevalent in the surrounding culture and who are too anxious to try their ideas out on a wider public. Ana-lytic work can be very lonely and isolating, and the only colleagues available to interact with may be those from the analyst's training body. This anomaly of the education process, in which the trained analyst remains a member of the closed group that trained her, encourages an adaptation to the ethos and theories of the training group and, contrary to the expressed aims of the institute, as a result stultifies the creativity of its members.

When I qualified as an analyst there was an accepted initiation into the group, involving formal assessments and interviews and then a reading-in of a clinical paper. Initiation is often spoken about as embedded in both the process and the end of the training, and, although the reading-in of the paper is more like a graduation process than an initiation, it does carry with it fear and anxiety about moving from one state to another. This view of initiation suggests that it is about the individual taking up his necessary place as an adult in society. Yet this does not include the idea that to be initiated could also be problematic for the individual because of the ambivalent feelings about what belonging may mean. Michael Balint suggests that initiation means a loss of individuality.

> We know that the general aim of all initiation rites is to force the candidate to identify himself with his initiator, to introject the

initiator and his ideals, and to build up from these identifications a strong superego which will influence him all his life. [Balint, 1948, p. 163]

In this sense, initiation means a giving over of the individual to the future service of the group and, although this provides an identity and a protected place to be, it might also encourage an unquestioning acceptance of the beliefs and aims of the group. After many hard years of training there may be a strong desire to be accepted beyond anything else. However, there is also inevitably a judgement associated with being seen fit to belong.

Soon after I finished my training, I dreamt that I was at the premises of my training organization and that I was too tall to go through the door. I say, "I must cut myself down to size". I seem to fear that to get through the door I have to become smaller. This dream could obviously be interpreted as displaying an inflated sense of self at having finally become an analyst. However, I see it as an expression of my anxiety that to fit in I would have to reduce myself in some way.

There is a danger implied in this process of initiation, which I believe is about the possibility of a self-betrayal: that the price to pay for gaining acceptance is to lose a capacity to be open to new and possibly dangerous creative paths. Hillman suggests that our fear of this capacity within ourselves is deeper than any other.

What we long for in life is not only to be contained in perfection by an other who can never let us down. It goes beyond trust and betrayal by the other in a relationship. What one longs for is a situation where one is *protected from one's OWN* treachery and ambivalence, one's own Eve. [Hillman, 1975, p. 65]

As I suggested in Chapter One, the image of Eve as the drive for change can be interpreted as a powerful source of creative female energy that we all fear. We would prefer to stay in the Garden of Eden where everything will remain the same rather than own our consciousness and our powerful capacity to initiate transformation. The capacity of the shadow side of the feminine can scare us all.

Against all the odds, considering how training organizations are structured, there can be an idealistic hope that change is possible. However, this is problematic, as change in structures and training would mean that members would have to face the masochistic submissions they had had to make to their own analysts and teachers and consider how these little deaths have affected their integrity and their work. It is, however, often the stated aim of training organizations to develop the individuality and creativity of its candidates, and to that aim to encourage talented applicants. The opposite is often true, that creativity is seen to be too unpredictable and risky.

> Therefore the artist, the philosopher, or the creative talent is a rare encounter within the creative team—too often being a bit too jumbled and unpredictable in a way which makes them a risk to the reputation of the profession. Professionalism rewards normality. [Reeder, 2004, p. 90]

Many talented people who have considered or have started training have given up the idea when they have experienced that the realities of training appear to be a form of indoctrination.

A profession which works with individuals to help them access healing and to creatively discover more about themselves, and which began with the sometimes wild, but eclectic talents of Jung, Freud, and Klein, has inevitably had to change to respond to public concerns and the requirement of statutory registration by the government. However, fears within the profession of being judged and found wanting have brought about a state of increasing self-restriction, which is a sad reflection of the inheritance of that creative turmoil a century ago. In 1996, Otto Kernberg published an important and deeply ironic paper entitled, "Thirty methods to destroy the creativity of psychoanalytic candidates". This paper presents a list of defensive measures by senior analysts against the threat of the unknown in their training candidates. He ends with the warning, "Always keep in mind: where there is a spark there may develop a fire, particularly when the spark appears in the middle of dead-wood: extinguish it before it is too late" (ibid., p. 1039). There can be a very powerful drive within institutes to maintain the dry wood at all costs and not to allow it to be changed by fire. The generational nature of institutes conspires against changes in the "family" ethos that has been passed down from analyst to analysand all the way back to Jung or Freud. This would be broken if the training of analysts was not tied up with membership of the training group. As in any other profession, other influences and filters would be allowed to come in and affect these archaic structures.

Much has been written about these confining aspects of analytic trainings and the conflicts raised in training institutes by the positions of power held by the training analysts (Allphin, 1999; Bruzzone, Casaula, Jimenez, & Jordan, 1985; Kernberg, 1986). Allphin (1999) looks at the powerful influences that dyadic relationships exert within training institutes. The South American psychoanalysts examine the influence of regression as a result of the power structure on their ability to function as analysts (Bruzzone, Casaula, Jimenez, & Jordan, 1985). More recently, Reeder has explored how these power issues also come to the fore within the training analyses themselves.

> . . . it would seem to be a matter of course that the candidates submission to and even identification with the forms of self reflection that are offered contribute to his "normalization" and gradual transformation into an acceptable colleague with the same language and convictions as the other members of the group he has chosen to be part of. [Reeder, 2004, p. 116]

There may be aspects of this "normalization" that are necessary and true for any professional training, such as for teachers, lawyers, or doctors; however, training to be a psychotherapist or analyst requires an ability to accept the unknown and a capacity to respond to this that is unique among professions. However, despite this, and maybe also because of it, there is a collective fantasy that there is one correct way of doing things. This "correct" way will, of course, vary between institutes, sometimes differing so dramatically from each other that training candidates and potential patients can become very confused about theoretical standpoints, with each group clinging to their own "true orthodoxy".

> *Orthos doxa*—the correct doctrine—is an intellectual instrument to keep oneself and others in check so that everything stays in accordance with the structure and the rule, which by dint of the immanent pedagogy, has become part of the professional superego. [*ibid.*, p. 207]

The status quo in the psychoanalytic world is based on a structure that has been reinforced by a superego position, which supports professional structures and theory and practice at the cost of change. In any situation in which habits and structures of a profession support a defensive and patriarchal framework, it is the feminine that will be attacked as dangerous, different, and other, and, as a result, both male and female members will suffer. Colleagues may long for a sense of mutual emotional support, but in an atmosphere of fear and envy it may not be possible ever really to say how one feels or even to trust one's closest colleagues. The need for a connection with the humanity as well as the creativity of the feminine, combined with the lack of sustaining and productive working relationships between colleagues (which is also a loss of the feminine), means that the analyst can easily feel isolated and forever on guard in case he or she is judged to be wanting.

Many years ago, in the euphoria of finishing my own training, I naïvely expected to be welcomed into the wider analytic community to which I now belonged. The first paper I submitted to a professional journal was on some thoughts about the training process I had recently been through. The response from the editor was encouraging about my writing, although she rejected the paper and suggested that she was "concerned" that I might need another analysis. She had no information as to whether I was in analysis at the time or not; in fact, she knew nothing about me and had never met me. The one thing she did know was that I had trained in a rival Jungian training to the one she belonged to. At the time I was able to see that this was an attack on my training organization as much as it was an attack on me, so I simply resubmitted the paper to another journal. However, with many years hindsight, I now believe that some of the attack was also about my "presumption" in the paper that a professional orthodoxy had its limitations. I had suggested that the fears generated by being an analyst and working closely with the unconscious could not be trained out of one; in fact that they should not be trained out of one but, rather, acknowledged as a constant in the work. One of the fears I wrote about was a fear of one's own destructiveness.

> We defend ourselves at all costs against our own ambivalence and self-deception. Yet acknowledging the loss and grief and pain of

this enables us eventually to change. I believe the profession as a whole has an ambivalent position towards this opening up. On the one hand candidates and colleagues are encouraged to know themselves, on the other hand there is a fear of both the destruction and the creative sparks that may be unleashed. [Miller, 2000, p. 64]

By challenging the status quo I was suggesting that in training we might be being encouraged to be defensive towards the unknown heart of the work because of both the creativity and destructiveness inherent in it. I also suggested that the purpose of training might encourage the candidate to become *less* sensitive to the patient's unconscious rather than more. This desensitization may be a more comfortable state to work in for the analyst, but results in an uncreative and schizoid professional—an analyst who can split herself off from the feelings generated in the room and watch herself working rather than being fully there.

Interpretation is one of the most powerful tools for therapists but it can easily become dangerous in the hands of the professional superego. We are trained to interpret what a patient means or what is going on for them unconsciously, and to use this expertise as a vehicle with valuable healing and creative possibilities—to use it, in fact, with love. But interpretation can be a double-edged sword and a powerful instrument for expressing hatred (Reeder, 2004, p. 210). Interpretation changes what is unfamiliar into something more familiar and digestible. It takes the position of "I know or I understand" rather than "I hear" or "I experience". Because of this power, it can be an enormously tempting to use it when talking to or about one's colleagues as well as one's patients. When used with hate it always reinforces the superior patriarchal position of "I know, and you don't, and you are therefore lacking in some way". Freud used it when speaking about Sabina Spielrein's work when he interpreted her work on destruction as an expression of her "ambivalence" rather than as a valuable idea. This is similar to saying "because you are a woman you are not allowed to think like this". This use of a patriarchal position, which in this instance would produce a theory to support the interpretation, is in effect pathologizing the feminine whether it is actually directed at a woman or not. This is Logos overpowering Eros by using language *about* the state, or affect, or situation rather than speaking *for* it. Love is absent when interpretation is used like this. The feminine in the woman is not being allowed to step beyond proscribed parameters, and if it does she is seen as *not complete* and as *other*.

This treating of the feminine as "lacking" if ideas or emotions are expressed that challenge the *orthos doxa* is not just rife within the literature but is prevalent between colleagues, be they male or female, and can be especially highlighted in the power relationships between candidates and senior colleagues. Much of this attack and fear of the feminine is deeply unconscious; the real shadow side of a profession which states its aims as exploring the unconscious of others. It partly comes from a cultural patriarchy, which was prevalent in the beginnings of the psychoanalytic movement and which has become more entrenched through theoretical views based on the mother–child dyad as an idealized image of the feminine, as I suggested in the previous chapter. However, I believe that it is also to do with the nature of what we, as analysts, do that has helped to drive this attitude towards the feminine into deeper areas of the unconscious.

Kernberg begins his paper on how to kill creativity in candidates by quoting a colleague, Lore Schacht. "Our problem is not so much to foster creativity but to try not to inhibit the creativity naturally stimulated by the nature of our work" (Kernberg, 1996, p. 1031). So, what is this creativity stimulated by the analytic work? In his study of alchemy, which Jung saw as a useful parallel representation of the analytic work, he suggested that the stage of *nigredo*, the melancholic immersion in the unconscious, was not just to be viewed and recorded by the alchemist but, far more importantly, to be *experienced* by him as a conflict.

> The *nigredo* not only brought decay, suffering, death and the torments of hell visibly before the alchemist, it also cast the shadow of its own melancholy over his solitary soul. In the blackness of a despair which was not his own, and of which he was merely the witness, he experienced how *it* turned into the worm and the poisonous dragon. . . . His work began with a *katabasis*, a journey to the underworld as Dante also experienced it, with the difference that the adept's soul was not only impressed by it but radically altered. [Jung, 1963, par. 493]

Jung was suggesting that the analyst or adept has to join the patient in the unknown, where there is both self-immolation and destruction. If this descent is submitted to, it will "radically alter" both people involved. Any patient who has experienced the strength of transference feelings and the power of archetypal forces stirred up in an analysis knows how these hold power for change. Similarly, any analyst who has experienced the extraordinary force of a patient's projective identification (when one is taken over by powerful feelings such as love, hate, anger, and betrayal, and believe them to be one's own) and had to work her way out of this, will appreciate the archetypal areas Jung is talking about. When under the influence of projective identification the analyst can "become" the patient. It is a deeply uncomfortable yet extraordinary way for the patient to communicate with the analyst and to say "feel how I feel". It is an accepted cliché of the profession that the analyst as well as the patient *is* altered by the work, but unless you are altered, transformation for the patient cannot happen.

This, I believe, is the creativity Lore Schacht is talking about (Kernberg, 1996), the creativity that comes about through an openness to a destruction of previous states of minds or identities. This openness to a semi-permanent state of fragmentation would be a stated part of any Jungian training. Some analysts refer to the training process and the analysis within it as a contained low-grade breakdown. One of the aims of the training process is to give the candidate the tools to help them contain these feelings, the idea being that, having gained some of the theory, it becomes easier to experience the fragmentation and lack of knowing without defending against it. But the suggestion that theory can help becomes a problematic issue when taken as a solution to the unknown. As Samuels suggests, the tendency of a training to protect the candidate from fragmentation and to concentrate on the idea of wholeness as a stated aim is counterproductive: "Wholeness exists before birth perhaps or after death. Wholeness is therefore a spiritual matter while fragmentation remains the affair of the psyche" (Samuels, 1981, p. 219).

It is when the creative possibilities of fragmentation, such as those experienced by Christiana Morgan through her visions, or by many women in analysis, elicit a fear of the darker feminine in the analyst that a defensive theoretical orthodoxy comes into play. For Jung, this took the form of interpreting Christiana's needs as ones to do with her relationship with her lover or himself rather than pursuing the powerful images of her internal journey. Potentially, Jung's theory of androgynous archetypes has the capacity to open up new areas of exploration for both men and women. However, instead of wishing to explore these radical possibilities, many psychoanalytic theories developed since Jung have simply reflected the anxiety of clinicians when presented with infinite possibilities of change and the unknown and have wanted to pin down more rigid subjectivities for both masculine and feminine. Jung himself also had a tendency to do this when he did not separate out his own projections about the feminine from actual experiences of his female patients.

Our longing for certainties and understanding will always have the effect of trying to fix psychological understanding about gender. However, Nina Coltart suggests that the work has to be based not on theory but on an act of faith:

> The act of faith may feel like a spontaneous regression to complete unknowing, and may well be accompanied by dread; it can be disturbing to the analyst and seem like a serious self-induced attack on his ego, which in a way it is. [Coltart, 1986, p. 191]

I am not suggesting that this fear of the unknown, which may be opened up by the work, is only experienced by male analysts. Female analysts can be as dogmatic and defensive as their male counterparts when presented with new forms that the feminine can move into. They may defend against a lessening of drive and an increase in nurturing in their male patients if they feel this threatens their own sense of femininity. Or they may constrain their fantasies about their female patients to fit their own theories of gender and unconscious prejudices. Early in my career I sometimes experienced a sense of restraint when a female patient expressed desires that I felt I had missed out on myself. My patients may have been trying to claim back characteristics projected on to men, such as aggression and sexual desire, and to explore these new feelings. I was aware of my envy at the time, but probably not so aware of my need to keep feelings about new subjectivities within an identity for the feminine that I had been taught and that I had introjected from a patriarchal framework. As Sue Austin says in her work on aggression, it is an "uncomfortable recognition that the very notions of identity that the analytic process offers are not only gross over-simplifications, but also circulate political ideologies" (Austin, 2005, p. 56).

When faced with a woman patient who may be attempting to explore areas of differing identities in herself, a therapist can hope to be open to these possibilities in the patient, or can fear these new identities and rush to the safety and "certainty" of theory and interpretation. This position of certainty can then become an expression of hate towards the patient. It is also a self-directed attack on the therapist's own capacities for empathy and understanding, and the result is that the humanizing elements of the relationship are lost.

It is most often in the mismanagement of the erotic transference of a female patient to a male analyst that the aggressive nature of the hate of the feminine is seen. Gabbard and Lester, in their book on boundary violations in psychoanalysis, detail the many forms that this can take.

> Under the rubric of sexual boundary violations, there is a diverse group of behaviors in which analysts may engage. At one end of the continuum are forcible rapes . . . At the other end of the continuum are verbal forms of sexual misconduct. One male therapist told his female patient that she was so sexy he could not help getting an erection in her presence. [Gabbard & Lester, 1995, p. 92]

Unfortunately, these boundary violations happen far more frequently than we wish to believe. This is, of course, true of many professional situations between men and women, especially those professions dedicated to the nurture and care of others. However, in these instances they reflect the patriarchy of society and the abuses of power inherent in this. Within analytic relationships these abuses can wound the psyche in ways that it is very difficult to recover from. We know from work on the sexual abuse of children and the intergenerational process of abuse within families that abuse of children affects their capacity to function normally and attacks their ability to symbolize (Sinason, 2002). When abuses happen within an analytic relationship it is as if the parental abuse of children is constellated, when a child may be told that the act of abuse is because that adult is the one who really loves and understands the child. The analyst may also feel that they are the only one who understands their patient. This fantasy may become a *folie à deux* that is treasured by analyst and patient alike.

This "love" fantasy may be at the core of much analytic abuse. Many analysts believe that love is in itself healing, and base their work and analytic attitude on this idea, that it is enough to love the patient, and that they will get better as a result of this love. A paranoid extension of this idea is that actual sexual intimacy between the analyst and the patient will also be healing. The sadistic origins of what Gabbard and Lester call "the therapeutic copulation fantasy" are often so unconscious or split off that the analyst will deny he had anything but the best of intentions for his patient and be oblivious to the harm he has caused. Like Jung's interpretation to Morgan that she needed a Siegfried to "break through her ring of fire", the analyst may interpret that the woman's fertility and creativity is entirely dependant on his own phallic interpretations. There are many more moderate forms of this fantasy, such as the analyst hanging on interminably to his patient, not allowing her to believe she is better because he cannot bear the loss of connection, or being so envious of the patient that he cannot go with her where she needs to go.

In their deep desire for a connection with the feminine, some male analysts will project their needs on to their female patients and interpret these as lacks in the patient rather than an expression of their own anima projections. This then becomes an attack on the feminine that they long for and feel they cannot have. These anima projections themselves may be one-sided and conservative in their expectations of what the feminine has to offer, rather than multi-faceted expressions and images of feminine subjectivities.

It is especially difficult for women to reject a submissive role in these situations when they may have lived all their lives with rejections of aspects of their feminine experience, and as a result may be unconscious of much of this. Some of the most difficult aspects to own might be those of aggression and feelings of hatred and sadism towards others. If these are disowned or rejected as not acceptable, a powerful energy for change is lost. As therapists, this loss will affect ourselves and our patients and will do nothing to challenge the structure of the profession.

For many women, their destructive desires are so unacceptable that they can only be experienced as impotent rage or acts of aggression against the self. Taboos against the accepting of destruction and aggression as part of the feminine psyche have to be overcome and accepted as part of the creative drive, and as an integral part of psychotherapeutic and psychoanalytic theories and framework.

In the next two chapters, I look at how two contemporary female sculptors have grasped their capacities for destruction and sadism and used them powerfully for their own creative journeys. These two artists do this in very different ways. One of them works and reworks areas of feminine vulnerabilities, thereby growing in her capacities to embrace both power and sadism as valuable female characteristics. The other embraces the destruction of form and meaning as a means of deconstructing and creating a powerful and unique expression of feminine artistic spirit.

PART IV

CREATIVITY AND ART

CHAPTER SEVEN

Power and vulnerability in the work of Louise Bourgeois

"I'm afraid of power: it makes me nervous. In real life, I identify with the victim, that is why I went into art. In my art, I am the murderer. . . . The process is to go from passive to active. As an artist I am a powerful person. In real life I feel like the mouse behind the radiator"

(Bourgeois, 1998, p. 227)

U ntil very recently, apart from a few notable exceptions, sculpture has been seen as a male domain. Women have more often chosen painting or drawing to express themselves in the fine arts. The three-dimensional aspects of sculpture, whether carved, sculpted, or constructed, use and take up space in a way that has been quite alien to accepted views of female creativity. The two sculptors I have chosen to examine in this and the following chapter have been able to step into new identities as creative women and take up space by harnessing their aggressive and destructive energies for their own ends. I believe they have a lot to teach us about how to wrestle and engage with the discontents of the creative feminine.

In this chapter I look at the work of Louise Bourgeois, a sculptor who explores issues of power and vulnerability and gender and sexuality, and through her work expresses a powerful individual feminine identity.

Louise Bourgeois, who was born in 1911 and is still working today, is recognized as one of the major figures in contemporary sculpture. Her large body of work spans a career of over seventy years, many of which were spent in relative obscurity. During the past twenty-five years she has gained an international reputation as a major independent force in the artistic community, and, at the age of ninety-five, she continues to explore new forms and to show her work in exhibitions around the world. She works in both two-dimensional and three-dimensional forms. Since the 1980s she has explored three dimensions through carved forms, moulded latex, metal structures, and found objects, and most recently she has been working with sewn and stitched forms. Her work is entirely auto-biographical and, whichever medium she is working with, her aim has been the consistent one of exploring feelings that are frequently uncomfortable and difficult to face. "It is not an image I am seeking. It's not an idea. It's an emotion you want to recreate, an emotion of wanting, of giving and of destroying" (Bernadec, 1996, p. 7).

Being able to connect with feelings, be it through thoughts or images, is central to an understanding of our internal emotional life. Young-Eisendrath proposes that this is the core of self-discovery.

> From all that I have learned about human development, through research, theories and the practice of psychotherapy, I would say that we must understand our emotions and the images connected to them in order to understand ourselves. Without this, we are likely to feel alienated, unknowable, isolated and adrift—a fairly good description of the existential and deconstructed versions of the human subject. [Young-Eisendrath, 2004, p. 79]

Bourgeois's work embodies this idea perfectly. She searches consistently for her own emotional truths through the making of structures and forms.

Since the 1980s, when Bourgeois's work was taken up by gallery owners, art critics, and the public, she has spoken and written widely about her early life and the influences on her art. Like her work, her words are often confusing, paradoxical, and ambivalent, but it is this ambivalence that is central to her identity as an artist and to the seductive and fascinating nature of her work for her public. She resembles no one else in the field and although she has been categorized by art critics as Surrealist or as Abstract Expressionist, she speaks of her work as "existential". In that she explores the pains of being a human in a world in which communication appears impossible, Bougeois does convey a sense of existential angst. This difficulty of communicating feelings is at the heart of her work. However, Bourgeois is not an artist to be categorized into any movement. She is an entirely independent creative feminine voice who, by working with her earliest memories and vulnerabilities on both a personal and archetypal level, has found a central place in the international artistic community.

Bourgeois' early childhood experiences are central to her work and frequently referred to by herself. For this reason it is important to have an idea of her early history. She was born in Paris, the second daughter of Louis Bourgeois, a tapestry merchant who bought, sold, and repaired tapestries. Louise was brought up surrounded by tapestries, needlework, and the intricate work of repairing. When she was born her father had wanted a son, and Bourgeois has said that a saving grace for her feminine self was that she did at least look like her father, so that there was some recognition from him even though she was female.

> I was the second daughter of a man who wanted a son. So to survive I had to create ways of making myself likeable. It was the only way of escaping the depression, which came from feeling superfluous—from feeling abandoned. Having been privileged with a native energy I switched from a passive role to an active one, which is an art that I have practiced all my life—the art of fighting depression (emotional dependence). [Bourgeois, 1998, p. 167]

Louis Bourgeois was a patriarch who ruled the household and looked down on women and their capacities. Two years after Louise was born the longed for son arrived. When Louise was ten her father employed a British woman, Sadie Richmond, to teach English to the children. This governess moved into the family home as a mistress to Louis, and the *ménage a trois* was in place for the remainder of Louise's childhood. Her mother suppressed her anger and did nothing to prevent this arrangement.

> Sadie, if you don't mind, was engaged to teach me English. I
> thought she was going to like me. Instead of which she betrayed
> me. I was betrayed not only by my father, dammit, but by her too.
> It was a double betrayal. [Gorovoy & Asbaghi, 1997, p. 35]

This betrayal, coupled with the earlier one of feeling unwanted as
a girl, resulted in states of isolation, abandonment, and a conviction
that she was unlovable. These emotional states have remained with
her throughout her life and been the foundation of her work.

Bourgeois has always maintained that these traumas are *central*
to her work as a sculptor, and that it is the continual working with
and working through of both the personal and collective unconscious which these traumas trigger and relate to that has kept her
sane. It is unusual for an artist to be so open about such early oedi-
pal and abandonment traumas, and to acknowledge them as the
driving force of her art. As a result, it would be easy to approach
Bourgeois's work entirely from a psychoanalytic perspective, for
which she gives ample material both in her work and in interviews.
However, by offering up these explanations herself, she has in a
way defused the power of interpretation for others. It cannot be
done to her because she has got there first. We have to accept that
her statement about her sources of creativity and drive to create are
true for her. "My childhood has never lost its magic, it has never
lost its mystery, and it has never lost its drama" (Bourgeois, 1998,
p. 1).

Although her willingness to talk about her childhood shows an
extraordinary openness to her most precious interior places, it has
also enabled her to have an identity or persona behind which she is
free to work. There is a tricksterish element at play here. We, as the
audience, can listen to the self-revelation and get absorbed in
connections and meanings while she gets on with her work. It
would be all too easy to take her interpretations of her psyche
entirely to heart, yet she herself suggests that this is not necessarily
a good idea.

> An artist's words are always to be taken cautiously . . . The artist
> who discusses the so-called meaning of his work is usually describ-
> ing a literary side-issue. The core of his original impulse is to be
> found, if at all, in the work itself. [*ibid.*, p. 15]

Her words are frequently contradictory and ambiguous, as is her sculpture, and in that way they both replicate the play of the unconscious and allow her identity to be fluid.

In 1938 Bourgeois married an American art historian, Robert Goldwater, and moved to New York. She has lived in the USA ever since. She had a few exhibitions in the 1940s, 1950s and 1960s, while bringing up three sons, and then had a long period of obscurity until she was rediscovered in the 1980s.

> It was just that I had the feeling that the art scene belonged to the men, and that I was in some way invading their domain. Therefore the work was done and hidden away. I felt more comfortable hiding it. [*ibid.*, p. 112]

Throughout this period she continued to work and to keep all of her creations. She has since said that this lengthy period of isolation enabled her to become the sculptor she is today. "My first experience of great luck was when I was not picked up by the art market and I was left to work by myself for about fifteen years" (*ibid.*, p. 144).

While keeping her early story in the background, what I would primarily like to explore here is the way in which, by harnessing the *power* of the creative act, she communicates feelings of vulnerability, pain, and anger that can be felt profoundly, both bodily and viscerally, by her audience. This capacity to communicate powerfully conscious and unconscious affects empowers her as an artist and enabled her to grow in strength as her career has progressed. "The mouse behind the radiator" grows into a powerful woman while retaining a persona as the traumatized artist. I do not intend to suggest that her early childhood experiences are not crucial to her creativity, but rather that through consistently reworking her relationship to her past she transcends the abandonment and isolation that is at the heart of her work. She does this through her unflinching capacity to explore the murderous as well as the loving feelings that are central to her work. I shall look at some of the significant aspects of her work chronologically.

The house

In 1946–1947, Bourgeois created a series of painted and drawn images entitled "Femme-Maisons" (Figure 3). The lower half of the

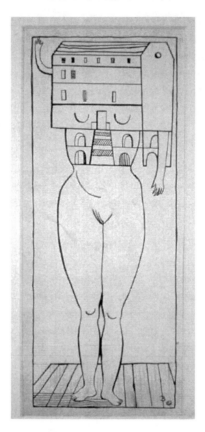

Figure 3. "Femme-Maison", by Louise Bourgeois, 1947 (ink on paper). Courtesy of the artist. Collection Solomon R. Guggenheim Museum, New York. Photo: Eeva Inkeri.

drawings depict a naked woman, the upper part a house. At the time, these were interpreted as feminist symbols depicting the demands of family and domestic life on a woman who was bringing up three children, but the images are more multi-layered than this, embodying as they do an inner psychic state of the importance of the original family houses of her childhood and the dramas that had been enacted therein. These first houses are engraved on Bourgeois's psyche and return in different forms throughout her work.

> The combination of geometric and organic forms, of rigidity and malleability, of architecture and viscera, serves as a metaphor for

her own psychic makeup. By visually and graphically uniting the two heterogeneous dimensions of woman and house, Bourgeois managed to overcome the dichotomy of mind and body, reason and emotion, analytic spirit and sensuality. [Bernardec, 1996, p. 23]

Primarily, the combination of house and body is shocking. Geometry meets sensuousness in a way that jars and disturbs. The idea of dismemberment as a lack of wholeness is introduced here and taken up in much later work in more violent ways. Commenting on these drawings later in her life, Bourgeois emphasized the women's vulnerability and lack of power.

> The woman is obviously nice looking, but she does not realize the effect she has on us. She does not know that she is half-naked, and she does not know that she is trying to hide. That is to say she is totally self-defeating because she shows herself at the very moment that she thinks she is hiding. [Gorovoy & Asbaghi, 1997, p. 98]

Here women's powerlessness and vulnerability is exposed.

Continuing the theme of lack of power, a series of engravings made at the same time, entitled "He Disappeared into Complete Silence" (Morris, 2003, p. 71), depict geometric houses and ladders based on tall New York buildings that, although in no way human, suggest human figures relating or not relating to each other. This building–person parallel is supported by the text, which tells of abandoned love, the destruction of a house, cannibalism, and a sense of being shut in. Commentators are often drawn to Bourgeois's work because of the explicitness and repetitiveness of the female struggle displayed there. Andrea Duncan suggests that it is difficult for a woman with a hypercritical father and a passive mother who endured her husband's adultery to find a solution to her psychic state, which is not the one of constantly reliving the original trauma through compulsive repetition. "Those ladders and scaffoldings are redolent of an opportunity never undertaken" (Duncan, 2003b, p. 87). There is a certainly a compulsive repetition in Bourgeois's work, of which she is very aware and fully exploits. Themes are repeated and returned to until everything has been said. Although these engravings can be read as a metaphor for her psyche, they are not drawings made by a patient in analysis, they are made to communicate with us. Bourgeois is using her creativity to empower her. It is her calling as an artist, which is central to her experience of being a woman.

> The inner necessity of the artist to be an artist has everything to do with gender and sexuality. The frustration of the woman artist and her lack of immediate role as an artist in society is a consequence of this necessity, and her powerlessness (even if she is successful) is a consequence of this necessary vocation. [Bourgeois, 1998, p. 99]

She seems to be suggesting here that, for women artists, the drive to create inevitably results in a sense of powerlessness. This search for a sense of power then becomes central to her work.

In the early 1930s, while she was in Paris, Fernand Leger persuaded Bourgeois that she was a sculptor rather than a painter, and, once she was married and settled in New York, she moved from drawing and engraving to making three-dimensional forms. She began carving structures in wood, tall elegant forms balanced precariously on tiny stands, or spiral forms made out of small pieces of wood attached to fine metal rods, which were pushed directly into the floor. These spiral works prefigure the hanging "Spiral Woman" of 1984 (Figure 4) and 2003 (Morris, 2003, p. 55), and are again a recurrent theme in her work.

> The spiral is an attempt at controlling the chaos. It has two directions. Where do you place yourself, at the periphery or at the vortex? Beginning at the outside is the fear of losing control; the winding in is a tightening, a retreating, a compacting to the point of disappearance. Beginning at the center is affirmation, the move outward is a representation of giving, and giving up control; of trust, positive energy of life itself. [Bernadec, 1996, p. 67]

The spiral is also a form representing the individuation process, as Bourgeois seems to suggest in its duality, repetition, and exploratory nature.

Body parts

During the 1960s Bourgeois produced some of her most obviously erotic objects, "Sleep 11" (1967), "Fillette" (1968) and "Femme-

Figure 4. "Spiral Woman", by Louise Bourgeois, 1984 (bronze with slate disc). Courtesy of the artist. Collection of the artist. Photo: Christopher Burke.

Couteau" (1969–1970). These sculptures embody the ambivalence of masculine and feminine and strength and weakness. "Fillette" (Figure 5), made from many layers of latex over plaster, is her best known piece, mostly as a result of the photograph by Robert Mapplethorpe of her wearing her monkey jacket and carrying "Fillette" under her arm, (Gorovoy & Asbaghi, 1997, p. 128). By calling the hanging sculpture of the male member, "Fillette" (little girl), she both denigrates and is tender towards the masculinity evoked. When confronted by interviewers she has consistently denied any aggressive motive. "When I carry a little phallus like that in my arms, well, it seems like a nice little object, it's certainly not an object I would wish to harm, that's clear. The niceness is directed towards men" (Bernadec, 1996, p. 78).

She does not, however, expect us to take this as the only feeling aroused, as is clear by the pose she struck for Mapplethorpe. It is she who is the one in control here. Bourgeois is, in psychoanalytic terms, taking a part object and imbuing it with meaning. Just as the baby does with the mother's breast, the part person signifies and

Figure 5. "Fillette", by Louise Bourgeois, 1968 (latex over plaster). Courtesy of the artist. Collection Museum of Modern Art, New York. Photo: © by Peter Moore.

incorporates the whole and this can be either good or bad, withholding or giving as experienced by the baby (Klein, 1988). However, this would be a very thin response to this multi-layered work if that was all we saw. "Fillette" communicates on many different levels. It is a symbol of fertility and virility, of Greek priapic myths, and, on a personal level, a reminder of the vulnerability of men as well as women: "I remember the model in life-drawing class at the Beaux-Arts getting an erection. He was embarrassed and I was amazed at how vulnerable he really was" (Bernardec, 1996, p. 81).

Bourgeois is also challenging the idea of artistic categories, as Roger Cook argues. "Thus there are constant erosions of fixed categories and distinctions (inside/outside, male/female, representational/abstract, organic/inorganic, aggressive/tender) to be found in her work" (Cook, 1999, p. 148). Dismemberment is a way of challenging our socially constructed views of sexuality and gender, and it allows her to play with our reactions and feelings generated by body parts which are unattached to a whole person.

"Sleep11" (Bernadec, 1996, p. 64), made in the previous year, is one of her most beautiful works. It is carved out of Italian marble and is an erotic form which, although phallic, suggests both male and female in its smooth, simple shape. Here, it seems there is no separate gender, male and female are one. The three stacked forms suggest simultaneously both a coming forth and a retreating. Bourgeois has interpreted it at various times as both a "self portrait" and "as a little animal recoiled in upon itself in order to gather its forces for waking up the next morning and starting again" (Bernardec, 1996, p. 82). She offers both a powerful and a vulnerable interpretation of the work. Maybe the beauty of the piece does lie in the sense of a lull in the struggle, or a momentary balance between masculine and feminine, power and vulnerability. The gender fusion is arresting, but also offers relief from the struggle between power and powerlessness.

"Femme-Couteau" (Figure 6), made in 1969–1970 out of pink marble, is again an erotic yet a more violent form than her previous work. The female body is eroticized, headless, and knife-like, "as though the entire eroticized body of a woman was the equivalent of a penis. The 'knife-woman' symbolizes defence and vulnerability" (Bernadec, 1996, p. 86). Here, the female is taking on some of the power and violence associated with the male to defend herself and her children, claims Bourgeois. Again, male and female attributes are combined; the woman is no longer the unconscious naked and vulnerable image of the "Femme-Maison", but she has inhabited a phallic form in its incarnation as power and aggression.

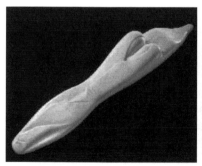

Figure 6. "Femme-Couteau", by Louise Bourgeois, 1969–1970 (pink marble). Courtesy of the artist. Emily and Jerry Spiegel Family Collection. Photo: Allan Finkelman.

Destruction of the father

The need to inhabit a phallic form to feel powerful changes dramatically with her next large work. In 1974, Bourgeois created a monumental work called "The Destruction of the Father" (Figure 7). This enormous latex structure is like a vast open mouth, or interior of a body. Most of the forms are spherical and smooth, maternal or phallic, but some are casts of chicken legs and joints of meat. This is a murderous work, full of rage and violence.

> This piece is basically a table, the awful, terrifying family dinner table headed by the father who sits and gloats. And the others, the wife, the children, what can they do? The mother of course tries to satisfy the tyrant her husband. The children are full of exasperation ... My father would get nervous looking at us, and he would explain to all of us what a great man he was. So, in exasperation, we grabbed the man, threw him on the table, dismembered him, and proceeded to devour him. [Gorovoy & Asbaghi, 1997, p. 142]

"The Destruction of the Father" evokes a claustrophobia that can only be overcome by murder and cannibalism. It becomes an

Figure 7. "The Destruction of the Father", by Louise Bourgois, 1974 (plaster, latex, wood, fabric and red light). Courtesy of the artist. Collection of the artist. Photo: Rafael Lobato.

oral drama. This work, showing the imagined vengeance on the father for his betrayal, his contempt for the female species, and his harshness against her as a female child, was made shortly after the death of her husband. It also, therefore, expresses the freedom that can come with the loss of "authority figures". There is a thrill to this sado-masochistic work where unacceptable social feelings are so violently expressed. Here, the feminine has no need of a power that belongs to the masculine, she has found her own, and, as Cook suggests, "Louise is determinedly *not nice*" (Cook, 1999, p. 150).

Bourgeois has spoken of what a crucial stage this marked in her ability to move on from her negative father complex.

> With "The Destruction of the Father", the recall was so strong, and it was such a lot of work, that I felt like a different person. I felt as if it had existed. It really changed me. That is the reason artists go on—it's not that they get better and better, but they are able to stand more. [Bourgeois, 1998, p. 158]

Although, as we can see in later work, the original affects and trauma are still used as the bedrock of her creativity, in this work she takes control and eats the object of hate, terror, and love. This is an uncomfortable work, and it rightly disturbs and upsets the viewer. This may be partly because Bourgeois is doing something that is seen as very unfeminine: she is taking control and exploring, not just our own uncomfortable relationship with the idea of cannibalism, but also touching on deep layers of the unconscious, where body parts, viscera, and the interiority of bodies affects us all. This is not acknowledged easily as female territory, or as an appropriate area of exploration for female artists. Jerry Gorovoy, who is a friend, in a review of Bourgeois's work, says this:

> . . . the provocative way her sculpture articulates what it is to be female makes it particularly challenging to the context through which importance and value are usually conferred. Her work deals with being a woman in a way that Freud could not have fathomed. It talks about things we don't want talked about, acknowledges forces we don't want broadcast loudly, and certainly not let loose. [Gorovoy & Asbaghi, 1997, p. 180]

In this way the work is not only an attack on her personal father but on our phallocentric society and the centrality of male meanings of rationality and logic. It is a subversive deconstruction through a view of the world as made up of body parts, which contain the power of meanings and feelings. Once both male and female bodies are deconstructed the social context of power relations can be redistributed or reinterpreted. As a woman, Bourgeois then has the power to eat as well as be eaten.

Cells

During the 1990s, when she was well into her eighties, Bourgeois produced some of her most challenging work with the "Cells". These are small rooms, constructed often from old wood and doors with symbolic and fetishistic objects in them. Here, she returns to the idea of the house as a metaphor for the body and juxtaposes internal and external, often returning to the claustrophobia and pain of trapped feelings. These are secret rooms, which we are allowed to gaze into as voyeurs. "The 'Cells' represent different types of pain: the physical, the emotional and psychological, and the mental and intellectual", (Gorovoy & Asbaghi, 1997, p. 196). In "Cell (Arch of Hysteria)" (1992) (Morris, 2003, p. 65), the arched body of a headless person expresses the hysterical merging of pleasure and pain. The sheet on which she/he lies has "Je t'aime" written on it over and over, as in a school punishment.

> It is a substitute for orgasm with no access to sex. She creates her own world and is very happy. Nowhere is it written that a person in these states is suffering. She functions in a self-made cell where the rules of happiness and stress are unknown to us. [Gorovoy & Asbaghi, 1997, p. 211]

In this work Bourgeois explores how affect stimulates bodies, what it does to a body's shape and structure, and how it seems to bypass the mind (the headless body). Confusingly, elsewhere, the body in this work is referred to by the artist as male, and the model for the body as Jerry Gorovoy, Bougeois's friend and assistant. "The hysteric is not a woman, as thought in the late nineteenth and early twentieth century, but a man, because men are hysterical too" (Bernardec, 1996, p. 137). This statement of Bourgeois's may relate to the ungendered state of hysterical affect; in effect, another dismembering of our cultural beliefs. In his book on hysteria, Christopher Bollas suggests that, "Hysterical theatre is always polymorphous as the self releases its sexual history in the devolution of becoming an event" (Bollas, 2000, p. 126).

Mother

During the past ten years, Bourgeois has moved on from working with affect around her relationship with her father and patriarchy as a theme, and returned to themes around her relationship to her mother and her own mothering capacities. The three towering constructions she made for the vast turbine hall when the Tate Modern opened its doors in 2000 are similar to her early drawings of buildings. The height of a small house, each construction invites the viewer to ascend a set of steps, at the top of which there is a platform with mirrors and a chair. She called this three-piece work "I Do, I Undo, I Redo" (Figure 8). Each column represents a state of mind. "I Do" is a positive, active state of a caring reflective mother. "I Undo" is the destruction of this state. Anxiety and guilt take over and passivity takes hold. "I Redo" is the movement towards a solution where there is activity again and reparation is possible. Here, the spiral reappears, and there is a working through of a problem or stage in life. As with the "Cells", the viewer is enticed into the structure, but this time, rather than being a voyeur, sees herself in the mirrors and uses herself as the affected object. The viewer is encouraged to be the body through which the affect is felt. Here, Bourgeois is asking us to think about how we see ourselves and reflect about our selves and our subjective states. When I visited this installation at the Tate, there were far more women and girls queuing up to ascend the towers than there were men. The promise of a new take on women's self reflective experience was obviously appealing. Bourgeois was encouraging her audience to think about themselves in a new way, stimulated by being within and central to one of her sculptures.

The other major work that she made for the Tate was an enormous spider made out of bronze, its legs straddling the bridge across the turbine hall. With this work and with the many other spiders she made during this period, she evokes her mother again

Figure 8. "I Do, I Undo, I Redo", by Louise Bourgeois, 1999. Installed in the inaugural exhibition of the Tate Modern in the Turbine Hall. (12.5.00 –26.11.00) Courtesy of the artist. Photo: Marcus Leith.

in the words she uses to describe her experience of spiders, "deliberate, clever, patient, soothing, reasonable, dainty, subtle, indispensable, neat". There is also a "tricoteuse" side to her, and she can be a "bit too fastidious" (Morris, 2003, p. 66). However, spiders, for Bourgeois, are beneficial and positive creatures. The positive elements of both these monumental works made for the Tate were a new departure. Here, reparation can be made both by the mother herself in recognizing and accepting her capacities for both love and destruction in the doing and undoing, and also within the symbol of the spider as mother. However, what these works communicated far more powerfully than anything else was the enormous size and energy of her forms, which took on the vast

Turbine Hall and appeared to fill it. Here was a woman taking up room and filling space with a freedom and abandon not usually associated with the feminine. As Austin suggests, for a woman to move freely within and take up space can be directly related to her experience of her aggression.

> In other words, the aggressive energies which have been split off in order to perform femininity well are likely to get stirred up in a woman who becomes an agent and makes use of space, rather than acting as a container of space for others. [Austin, 2005, p. 149]

These were works of an artist at the height of her powers who no longer feels that she has to hide her work away from the male art establishment or struggle with images of "Femmes-Maisons". She has earned her place on her own terms. "A woman has no place as an artist until she proves over and over that she won't be eliminated" (Bourgeois, 1998, p. 97). When she first exhibited at the Tate, Bourgeois was in her late eighties, and it was clear that she was taking advantage of the extraordinary creativity of old age with a new freedom to go exactly where she wished in her relationship with the unconscious.

Sewing and stitches

In her most recent work, Bourgeois has returned to the craft she learnt at her mother's knee, where she was instructed in stitching and repairing tapestries. Much of this new work consists of small stuffed figures displayed in glass or metal cases, enacting out emotions or states of mind. These narratives are underpinned by the weaving, sewing, and repairing that Bourgeois learnt in her childhood. The archetypal is powerfully present here. Pink stuffed and sewn figures locked together in a multiple embrace, many double-headed, stir up early childhood traumas in us, which we may wish were more deeply buried. There is a confusion of limbs and bodies here and a worrying sense of erotic merging (Morris, 2003, p. 41). In a more direct relationship to mythology the glass case containing "Oedipus" consists of a series of pink stuffed figures depicting the relationship of the bodies involved in the stages of the story (*ibid.*, pp. 44–45).

Some of the most beautiful of these stuffed and sewn works are the tall precarious columns of stuffed cushions, balancing, seemingly impossibly, on the smallest form. The fusion of architecture and bodies, which she first explored with her "Femme-Maison" are here reworked into an artistry of soft towers (*ibid.*, pp. 48–49). However, the most arresting of all these stuffed works are the tapestry heads, which stare at us from glass cases. They are crudely sewn yet carefully sculpted forms that suggest Egyptian mummies or totemic figures. With their mouths open to express pain or fear, they are cut off from us behind glass and perfectly communicate the existential human condition (*ibid.*, pp. 38–40). There is both a terror and a beauty to these heads, which engage with the audience on a visceral level. Power and vulnerability are here merged, as are male and female and the present and the past. Through her intense and unflinching feminine relationship to her work, which involves archaic struggles between male and female and power and vulnerability, Bourgeois is able to connect to a level of human experience that is free from gendered and cultural accretions. I would suggest that her overt struggles with patriarchy and her unflinching ability to face her own sadism and her murderous and vengeful feelings has enabled her, at this late stage in her life, to explore a whole new level in her work. This level is what Arthur Miller has called, "an aesthetic of the mind's deep layers" (Gorovoy & Asbaghi, 1997, p. 216).

To a certain extent, this "aesthetic of the mind's deep layers" mirrors Jung's view of the artistic process.

> The creative process, so far as we are able to follow it at all, consists in the unconscious activation of an archetypal image, and in elaborating and shaping this image into the finished work. By giving it shape, the artist translates it into the language of the present, and so makes it possible for us to find our way back to the deepest springs of life. [Jung, 1996b, p. 82]

However, Jung was not aware of the additional struggles that women have to face in making creative connections to these deep layers. As I have suggested, Bourgeois does this by overtly taking on the struggle *for* the feminine and exploring it in all its vengeful, sadistic, and murderous aspects, as well as its loving ones. It is this exploration that makes her powerful, but she also does not ever lose sight of the powerlessness of "the mouse behind the radiator", which has been with her since her early "Femmes-Maison" drawings, and both of which now come together in her extraordinary existential late work.

CHAPTER EIGHT

Creative destruction in the work of Cornelia Parker

"People find it quite weird that women make violent work, or work that uses violence. But we have as much right to it as anyone else"

(Parker, 2004)

Cornelia Parker is a British sculptor with a unique relationship to matter and the interiority of matter. Her work has the capacity to act as a powerful projective screen for the viewer and to encourage internal conversations. She questions our relationship to things and to the psychic space that things take up. She transforms matter to show us that nothing is finite and all will eventually be burnt, buried, lost, and returned to that from which it came. She achieves this through aesthetically beautiful micro and macro forms, which can challenge and tease us and have the power to be spiritually moving. However, what Parker also shows us is something about feminine artistic exploration and imaginative power, which, in its use of and delight in the anarchic destruction of matter, enables a powerful individual spirit to be expressed.

Cornelia Parker is now in her late forties, and since her twenties has exhibited extensively in the UK, Europe, and the USA. However, she stands apart from the main artistic community of today and is fiercely independent of bland media stereotypes. "I don't want to make work which fits into any category. I can't be lumped in with any movement. I want to be free" (Parker, 2004). She brings to her work aspects of her religious upbringing as a Roman Catholic, her northern roots, her early fascination with science, and, inevitably, her own personal story, but these are all small inputs into the main creative drive which, I will suggest, brings untapped aspects of the feminine imagination into the centre of modern artistic and cultural thought. Although Parker thinks of herself as an artist rather than a female artist, she acknowledges that there is an expression of the feminine in her work. "I don't necessarily think about my gender when I am making works. Obviously it comes out, they are quite feminine works, but I don't make it conscious" (Parker, 2004).

I shall consider some of the themes in her work that have challenged me as a therapist to think more deeply about the source of feminine creative drives, and how the "forbidden" emotions of aggression and destructiveness may hold a key to enable women to access these drives more directly. Cornelia Parker's work unashamedly harnesses destruction for its own creative ends, and despite, or maybe even as a result of, her independent stance, she has carved out a place in the centre of today's artistic community. Parker's work is neither marginalized as "women's art" nor has it been subsumed into passing cultural elites or trends. It stands powerfully and strongly in its own right as a statement of focused feminine creative energy.

In looking at her work, I shall divide it loosely by using the words that she uses to label it – "exploding", "exhaling", "stretching", "squashing", "The Maybe" and "the subconscious of".

Exploding

One of the first works that brought Parker strongly into the public eye was made in 1991. "Cold, Dark Matter: an exploded view", is now in the permanent collection at the Tate Modern (Figure 9). This

Figure 9. "Cold, Dark Matter: an exploded view", by Cornelia Parker, 1991. Courtesy of the artist, Tate Modern and Frith Street Gallery.

sculptural installation is introduced to us first as a photo of an ordinary-looking garden shed, which is then followed by a structural form made up of suspended fragments of the same shed, which has undergone an enormous explosion. Each piece from the destroyed shed and its contents is hung around a naked light bulb. Broken pieces of wood hang next to parts of garden implements and other ordinary objects. The entire piece moves gently with the movement of air in the gallery.

This piece throws shadows on the walls, ceiling, and floor, and has the capacity to evoke many images; an exploded diagram like those from a children's encyclopaedia, or a constellation of planets and stars, hanging around a central sun or moon. The ordinary bottom of the garden, the place for traditional male withdrawal and absorption, has been transformed, by losing its solidity, into a thing of lightness.

> A moment of suspension, reorganized precariousness, traces of destruction, the image retains the moment of the explosion, freezing it in its dissolution before it potentially disappears altogether ... the fragments speak to us with all their eloquence about the

oblivion of the original image and of the worlds opened up by their rearrangement. [Antich, 2004]

To help in the destruction of the shed, Parker enlisted the British Army's school of ammunition and had a controlled explosion performed. The destroyed pieces were then carefully gathered together and brought back to the exhibition space, where they were suspended on wires. In asking the army to help her with this explosive act, Parker engaged with an authority figure to enable her to be creative. "I was kind of subverting my fear by asking them to help me rather than do the opposite . . . and you have some common ground even if it is very tenuous" (Parker, 2004). The army has been shanghaied into a creative act. Parker is bringing together the violence of the munitions unit, her own and our exultations in explosions, and then transforming that into a still moment frozen in time, which is not only aesthetically pleasing but also spiritually moving.

This work echoes her ongoing fascination with "Matter and what it means", which is the title Parker took from a child's encyclopaedia of the 1950s and which she gave to an earlier work. In "Cold, Dark Matter" there is both bravery and power in the way in which Parker grasps her material and throws it up in the air and rearranges the world. This is a feminine creativity, which seems to say, look, everything can be different, nothing is stable. There is no consistency in the world, but there is a lightness to matter that we forget about. Although there are echoes here of modern physics' absorption with matter and how it is made up, and the spiritualization of matter that the alchemical process attempts to achieve, this sculpture does not directly reflect an interest in physical and chemical processes, but rather an exultation of delight in how we can change our perceptions of the things that surround us by breaking them up.

> By trying to unpick or dismantle something and remake it, somehow the perimeters get changed. What I'm trying to do is take very clichéd monumental things, things that everyone knows what they are (or you think you know what they are) and then trying to find a flip side to it or the unconscious of it. [Parker, 2000, p. 46]

By remaking the world or objects within it, Parker suggests to us that this is the way to understand more about both ourselves and our relationship to the world. She encourages us to give up our fixed ideas, to let our imagination run riot, and to upend received, perceptions. She presents us with a destroyed and transformed object, which encourages multiple projections in the viewer and then draws them into a creative process with her.

By challenging the way in which art is made, Parker is able to challenge the patriarchal structures that have formed artistic ideas. Rozsika Parker and Griselda Pollock, in their book on feminism and art, explored the idea that without a change in the way art is made it is not possible to challenge these structures (Parker & Pollock, 1987).

This process of destruction is an exciting one to engage in; it gives us a new way of thinking about feminine imaginative power and where it might go if it is allowed new forms to move into. It does not fit into the gendered assumptions of the feminine, which are allied to image and emotions, to the female artist as inexorably connected to the domestic and the relational, and nor does it fit in with the corruption of these, which has been traditionally associated with the witchlike feminine. By this I mean that if women's art is only allowed the categories of domestic and relational, or expressed through the corruption of these, then it is always marginalized. Parker's work opens up a third option, an intelligence that breaks through, or maybe even disregards gendered assumptions or attacks on these assumptions. Instead, her work engages the transcendent function and expresses the feminine as both spirit and matter, as both image and the "Big Bang" (Morgan, 2000, p. 22). There is an anarchy here that harnesses the destructive act purely for its own creative ends and triumphantly celebrates this. This is not aggression against self, or fear of aggression against the other, as is so often experienced by women in a relational sense, both of which can become dead ends. This aggression becomes the transformative synthesis and the creative drive, which then opens up new possibilities. Instead of seeing this aggression as abnormal, as much psychodynamic theorizing of gender would do, Parker encourages us to see that this is normal. This is not the anger that is stereotypically understood in much psychoanalytic writing as the enraged anger of the woman as other or inferior, but a harnessing of aggression, which is freely available to both genders.

In "Cold, Dark Matter: an exploded view", Parker shows us that there is a capacity of the female artist to use what have frequently been seen as male gendered forms of destruction for powerful effect to create a thing of light and brightness. In that sense, she suggests that there is a place for the creative feminine in the materialization of spirit and the capacity this holds for intellectual thought. "Cold, Dark Matter" had such a powerful effect on a cleric of St Paul's Cathedral that he based his Easter sermon on it and what was happening in Iraq.

> What he did was take the whole congregation out of the church and across the [Millennium] bridge to see my piece [in the Tate Modern]—the whole St Paul's Cathedral full of people—and I thought this was amazing. So he's obviously using it for his own dialogue in bad world politics. [Parker, 2004]

Squashing

During the period of time in which she was making "Cold, Dark Matter: an exploded view", and "Thirty Pieces of Silver" (Figure 10), for which she squashed and rolled out quantities of silver plate, Parker was living in a house that was due to be knocked down for a motorway. The threat of demolition lasted ten years, and in interviews she gives this as the background to her work of the time. However, since the late 1980s she has returned again and again to similar themes in which she squashes silver objects. In 2001, she was commissioned to make "Breathless" (Figure 11), for the Victoria and Albert Museum. The squashed silver wind instruments hang in a circular space between the ground and first floors of the new British Galleries. The piece can be seen from above and below. It is suspended on fine wire from the ceiling and all the pieces move slightly in the air.

Parker has transformed wind instruments into flattened images of their former selves. This, like all her pieces, is witty, and emphasizes this in its title, "Breathless". She also plays with our sense of magic and, like Uri Geller, makes us wonder how the bending or squashing has happened. For her original squashed piece, "Thirty Pieces of Silver", Parker enlisted the help of a steamroller, which often entirely destroyed the silver object. Now she does the squashing herself with a 250-ton industrial press, which flattens the silver

Figure 10.   "Thirty Pieces of Silver", by Cornelia Parker, 1988–1989. Courtesy of the artist and Frith Street Gallery.

Figure 11.   "Breathless", by Cornelia Parker, 2001. Courtesy of the artist, the Victoria and Albert Museum and the Frith Street Gallery.

objects into cartoon drawings of their former selves. If they are broken up she throws them away. The caption for "Breathless" includes a description by her of how the squashing for this piece was done.

> Breathless takes the form of a hypothetical brass band, a collection of defunct instruments acquired from the dusty backrooms of the British Legion, Salvation Army, collieries and other establishments. No longer played, these horns shared the fate of being squashed by the weight of one of our most famous historical monuments, Tower Bridge. The deed was done by one of the giant 22 ton accumulators, part of the bridge's original hydraulic lifting mechanism. One Victorian institution literally knocked the wind out of another. [Parker, 2001a]

There was some anger expressed by a brass band enthusiast about this piece when it was first installed but it has since been proudly embraced by others and is emblazoned on the cover of a recording of brass instruments. It seems that even for those for whom the original objects are precious, the destroying of their form is seen as transformative.

We could think of Parker's art as being an extension of Winnicott's idea of the necessity of the infant being able to own the aggressive gesture if she is to develop and grow; that the first aggressive reaching out is an act of self-realization, which helps to instil in her a positive sense of aliveness, linking the spontaneous gesture to the idea of the true self and creativity (Winnicott, 1992b). However, as I have been arguing, I believe women's struggle for creative expression is a more complicated issue than the simple beauty of Winnicott's idea suggests. Women's creative expression has a tendency to end up either as marginalized or pathologized as dark and witchlike. For women to engage with their creativity fully, something has first to be broken.

In her paper on the potential for a subversive and imaginative role for Miranda in *The Tempest*, Marie Angelo suggests an alternative route for feminine creative drive and proposes "an image of feminine imaginative power which is neither corrupt, nor the creator of monstrosities, nor isolated from the mainland psychologies of reason and intellect". Angelo calls this, "this thing of brightness, I acknowledge mine" (Angelo, 2003, p. 119). She is proposing a new way of thinking about female imagination and creativity, which she refers to as, "not hard science, but hard art" (*ibid.*, p. 142).

I would suggest that "hard art" is an appropriate term to use to describe Parker's art. There is an expression of the self in Parker's work that shows itself as a "thing of brightness" and speaks as an independent creative voice. It is part of my argument to suggest that it is because of her use of violence and destruction in her work that she is able to express herself so fully. By embracing her aggressive fantasies she breaks the link with culturally accepted forms of female creativity and finds instead a new creative path.

The transgressive nature of this act is crucial in enabling the woman to temporarily release herself from gendered constraints. Acknowledging and owning aggression can have a transformative effect and help to break through the overarching relational aspect that cloaks women's self experiencing.

By beginning the work by physically destroying her chosen materials, Parker is breaking that first relational link to the object and trusting that if she lets go of old meanings and forms, new ones will appear. For "Still Life with Reflection", 2004 (Figure 12), she has suspended silver coffee pots and candelabras with a reflective

Figure 12. "Still Life with Reflection", by Cornelia Parker, 2004. Courtesy of the artist, St Bartholomew's Hospital and Frith Street Gallery.

pool of the squashed object at right angles to the three dimensional one.

> So you get some clapped out old teapot which has had as much use as it can probably bear and now it's on its last legs and it's going to be destroyed anyway and I tip it finally into the grave and resurrect it again, so that it becomes art or alter ego. That's very cathartic. [Parker, 2004]

The suspended silver objects and their squashed reflections are not only aesthetically beautiful, but stimulate a host of questions in the viewer.

> Her combination of object and language and the often-violent fate that she imposes on her raw materials are all carefully chosen for their powers of deconstruction and reconstruction. Cognisant of our capacity for projection, Parker encourages the audience to question conventions. [Morgan, 2000, p. 16]

This capacity of Parker to encourage an internal conversation in the viewer is crucial to an appreciation of her work. Viewing her pieces may start as an aesthetic experience, but this soon transforms from an appreciation of image into an awareness of process. When Parker first began making sculptures, she used some of the sculptor's stock in trade, plaster, paper, wire, materials that were as lacking in reference as possible, but she soon gave this up to start working with the most loaded material and things she could find, "the most recognized, the most clichéd thing. They are clichéd for a reason. There is immediate recognition" (Parker, 2004). Parker makes us reassess our tendency to accept things as they are. She encourages a questioning about what has happened to these objects and a realization that they can mean whatever we want them to mean. Our capacities for projection and our desire to do so are encouraged and exploited by the artist and our expectations are constantly questioned. If a squashed silver coffee pot can be a shadow, or a pool, or an alter ego, or a tragi-comic cartoon character, what does that mean for the rest of the material world and how substantial is it really? As a child, Parker used to squash precious pocket money coins on the railway track. "You couldn't spend your pocket money afterwards but you kept the metal slivers for their own sake, as an imaginary currency and as physical proof of the destructive powers of the world" (Parker, 2000, p. 16). It was also at this point in her childhood that Parker may have been learning about her own potential for power in her acts of destruction and, therefore, her capacity to own her own sense of agency, an essential tool in the creative process.

When installing her most recent work, "Still Life with Reflection", in the waiting room of the cancer clinic in St Bartholomew's Hospital in London, Parker was concerned that the obvious associations to removed breasts or flattened, X-rayed breasts might upset the women. However, this was not the response to this imaginatively challenging piece of work, which hangs as a line of silver objects and their reflections from the high ceiling of the statuesque waiting room. The response was rather one of humour and delight. "I just can't take my eyes off it", "It's the cash in the attic", "It makes you laugh, how could you put any fruit in that bowl?" (Carpenter, 2005, p. 4).

Parker's work has transformed the waiting room, a place of anxiety, illness, and darkness, into an ethereal delight, a place for enjoyment and contemplation. Her daring work opens up new possibilities for the waiting patients. "... we might speculate that something emerges in women's aggressive fantasies which might have potential to touch levels of awe, horror, power, fascination and ecstasy which have traditionally been regarded as religious experiences" (Austin, 1999, p. 25).

Stretching

Parker is immersed in the traditional world of the sculptor, of matter and materials, but she broadens that out beyond image and touch. "There's the metaphoric, psychoanalytic idea of materials and what they mean and there's the scientific idea and historic idea of what materials mean. It depends on which context that material is in" (Parker, 2004).

One of her worked and reworked relationships to materials is in stretching them. Here, she literally stretches the idea of what materials mean to us and how we could imaginatively think about them. "Measuring Niagra with a Teaspoon", made in 1997, is exactly that, a Georgian teaspoon melted down and then drawn out to a fine thread, which measures the height of the Niagara Falls. "Measuring Liberty with a Dollar" (Figure 13), made a year later, is a fine coil of silver thread drawn out to the height of the Statue of Liberty.With stretching, she again starts with the necessity of first breaking her object up. Destruction is the door through which the imaginative leap can be made. The destruction frees us from old ways of seeing and allows us to access new thoughts and ideas. With stretching, she returns again to the idea of lightness, which is so prominent in her suspended work and also draws us into ideas of small and large and questions our assumptions about what can be measured with what. Does the spoon really measure the height of Niagara, or are we being seduced into that idea? Normal conventions are thrown aside and we are back in the child-like world of squashed coins, pieces of string and a delight in the minute or the gigantic. Her desire to destroy her material and transform it into something else is there in the wire drawings.

I want to do a piece with crucifixes and have it called "Beyond Belief". So I melt down crucifixes and have them made into

Figure 13. "Measuring Liberty with a Dollar", by Cornelia Parker, 1998. Courtesy of the artist and Frith Street Gallery.

wire. The idea that they have been made by man and the idea of destroying it, like turning a cross into a line, so it's undoing the symbol somehow. [Parker, 2004]

Parker is consistently saying to us, *do not take what you see for granted*. Something like a crucifix, that we respond to from layers of cultural and sociological associations, can be transformed, or deconstructed, and become something else. It may consist of the same matter, but can be read in an entirely different way. Meaning is movable, changeable, and can, in the terms of physics, be both a particle and a wave. Parker's work makes it very hard for us to stay with certainty or presume anything. A process of engagement has to be entered into; nothing can be taken for granted as we are taken down a road without answers but which opens up the world to us in a variety of new ways.

The Maybe

The sense of challenging the accepted is there in her 1995 installation "The Maybe". In this work, she questions our reactions to cultural iconic items by framing and enclosing them. This installation, in the Serpentine Gallery in London, attacks our unquestioned cultural assumptions about the objects that surround us and whether we see them as dead or alive. The central piece of the installation was the actress Tilda Swinton asleep in a glass case. Other objects were a blanket and pillow from Freud's couch, a scrap of Lindberg's plane, the brain of Charles Babbage, Queen Victoria's stocking, Charles Dickens's quill, and other culturally liminal objects (Morgan, 2000, pp. 31–33). Visitors to the gallery were made nervous by their awareness of a *living*, semi-famous person in a glass case, surrounded by other *dead* objects. "Parker clearly views these objects as ripe for projection and interpretation and rescues them from languishing uncreatively in the sterile environments of their more conventional museum surroundings" (*ibid.*, p. 34).

It is as if Parker is saying that there is more life in these well known objects, a culture of the unconscious that we have to look for and listen to.

I was trying to find cultural archetypes right across the board. . . .
But it is more like trying to build an exquisite corpse from all these
little fragments. We have the remains of this culture but all these
people have gone, Freud, Victoria, Dickens, we have these isms
which inform our language . . . but it is more like trying to look at
it in a more intuitive way and feel it because it *is* a physical material. You physically hold a feather in your hand that has heard as
much as Freud and somehow try to make that speak for itself.
[Parker, 2004]

We are left with the question, does the feather have anything to say?
Should we treat this as an exquisite object or not? Parker has always
been fascinated with meaning-laden objects like the Turin Shroud.
"Whether it's a fake or not doesn't really matter. It's got that reso-
nance for people. That's what fascinates me about materials"
(Parker, 2004). She has expressed a desire to visit Lourdes, simply
to soak up the heady atmosphere of projected beliefs and meanings.

Exhale

Projections are expressed in a different form in Parker's "exhaled"
works. "Western art is mostly about the opposite of breathing, the
lack of breath" (Parker, 2004). If in the West we are inclined to hold
things in for fear of losing them, then exhaling may be an important lesson about the creative space this leaves. "Breath of a
Librarian", made in 1998, is a burst balloon that was discovered in
the reading room of The British Library. Here she suggests both the
captured breath once inside the balloon and the lack of it, but also
the idea of the breath that is still there in the form of the deflated
balloon.

In her "exhaled" works, Parker teases us with the idea of the
creative breath and with her belief that "the unconscious has a
devilish way of having its out" (Parker, 2004). In "Exhaled Blanket",
made in 1996 (Figure 14), dust and fibres from Freud's couch are
trapped in a glass slide and then projected. The microscopic view
of hairs and dust particles, and who knows what other blown-up
minutiae from Freud and his patients' breath and skin and hair, is
aesthetically beautiful and, like "Cold, Dark Matter: an exploded
view", suggests macro worlds through a micro one. "Exhaled

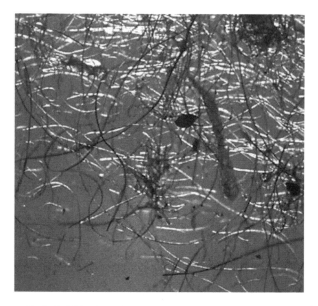

Figure 14. "Exhaled Blanket", by Cornelia Parker, 1996. Courtesy of the artist and Frith Street Gallery.

Cocaine", made in 1996, is a pile of brown incinerated cocaine (Morgan, 2000, p. 43). By thanking HM Customs and Excise, Parker encourages in us a process of questioning, both about her relationship with Customs and Excise and our responses to a pile of now useless and destroyed mind-altering drugs, no longer to be inhaled.

By broad use of the words inhale and exhale, Parker wonders about our relationship to what we take in and push out. "Inhaled Cliffs" consists of a neat pile of white sheets starched with chalk from the white cliffs of Dover. "Exhaled Schoolhouse" is a photo of a school building in Glasgow completely covered in small chalk marks (*ibid.*, p. 55). "It was almost like an accumulation of all this chalk exhaled through the walls, marking time. It was ephemeral, because it washes away. It was almost like a way of dematerializing the school building, another institution" (Parker, 2000, p. 57).

The subconscious of

I trust my subconscious more than my conscious. The whole point about work is to let it tell you something. So basically the work is just the way to read perhaps a visual model of the way your mind works or the externalization of something, so that I can look at it and say "Oh that's interesting". I see it and I read it but I forget it somehow. I can say "Oh that's happened". A mechanism to feel as free as possible in the work. [Parker, 2004]

This is also what she offers us, a chance for us to see how we respond. "Marks made by Freud subconsciously" (Figure 15), made in 2004, is a macrophotograph of the seat of Freud's chair. It looks like the hide of an elephant or an aerial photograph of the desert, but the most powerful projections we may bring to this photo are those to do with the image of where Freud sat day in and day out, the imprint of his bottom. There is almost a sense of the sacriligious here, and yet through this act she is reconnecting us to the idea that Freud was both simply and physically a man, as well as a great thinker.

In "Subconscious of a Monument", 2001, soil removed from under the leaning tower of Pisa to prevent it from falling down is suspended at body height from wires across the width of a room (Antich, 2004, p. 41).

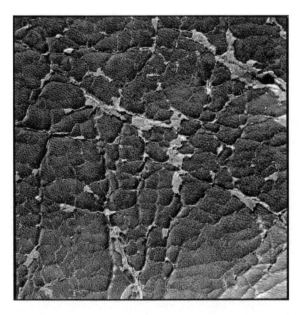

Figure 15. "Marks made by Freud subconsciously", by Cornelia Parker. Courtesy of the artist, the Freud Museum and Firth Street Gallery.

I'm trying to find uncharted territory in the most visited spot or idea, trying to find space where things are the most crowded. It's like going to the eye of the storm. In the shadow of these monuments or icons, there must be the most unstable things in our society, the things that we can't map. And as individuals we have that too. [Parker 2001b]

It is here, in the uncharted and unstable territory of both mind and matter, where Parker encourages us to explore the edges and slippages of identity. This is the borderline where roles and meanings are not proscribed or set. As she is aware, this is a shaky place where both the trickster and the devil abide, and where it is hard for us not to yearn for certainty. "We got married on Brooklyn Bridge, and our wedding photo shows us and the Twin Towers. We wanted that symbolism because we thought it might be an enduring monument, and a few years later it disappeared!" (Parker, 2004).

Throughout her work, Parker is trying to show us how crucial it is to find connections and channels to the unconscious because it has so much to teach us about how we respond to and view the world, and about how narrow that view is. She creates as many channels as she can to encourage the unconscious to show its symbols and express itself. By breaking and destroying, Parker shows "the devilish way" the route to take. It is as if she bursts a dam or breaks a container to encourage the unconscious and her creativity to flow freely. She does not set out with fixed intentions in her work, but attempts to be constantly open to the process. "I think intention is just a decoy. It's just a strategy to get you on a journey from A to B but what you find on the journey is something else . . . the idea is just a kind of skin" (Parker, 2000, p. 59).

Parker's "hard art" is an expression of feminine imaginative power, which follows no rules and is not constrained by proscribed female identities. By using the idea of destruction as central to her work, she has made a break from any easy identifications and categorizing and has arrived at a place where she is recognized as a central figure in the contemporary art scene. She has done this by using aspects of the female self that are mostly unacknowledged and unaccepted as important parts of feminine identity and creativity.

Conclusion

Women's discontents with their creative capacities may be extensive and are not easily resolved, resulting as they do from such a multitude of historical, social, and psychic factors. Each woman will find her own way to negotiate through these to a place where she can be creative. However, there is a factor that, I believe, may be crucial to this successful negotiation, and that is the ability to acknowledge and use a capacity for aggression. The acceptance and understanding of the positive aspects of aggression can bring about a change in a woman's self-experiencing, for by doing so she steps into uncharted territory.

By looking at the work of Louise Bourgeois and Cornelia Parker, I am suggesting that this welcoming and using of aggression may be the crucial element that enables creative women to step into a new identity, which is free from the discontents enumerated by this book. Both of these sculptors inhabit a world that has been restructured by themselves, free from cultural and gendered restraints. Bourgeois does this by using and exploring her own fight with patriarchy. Through a long and evolving process of repetition and struggle she eventually finds a way through to deep layers of the psyche, which are common to both men and women. Parker approaches the problem differently, by destroying the form of her artistic materials and thereby destroying their contexts and meanings. She then makes us look at things in a new way without our previous cultural and artistic baggage.

Both sculptors use their aggression to bring about change, one in relation to people, by working and reworking close family relationships, and the other in relation to matter by destroying and transforming it. They both appear to appreciate the importance and energy of this destructive aspect of their feminine selves and welcome its need to be expressed. Instead of fighting with it or denying it, they open the door to this darker and more unknown part of their psyches and meet their creative "daimon" face on. By doing this they may not be experienced as "nice", but they get to the place they want to be where they can be fully creative. These two sculptors challenge the *forms* of the artistic practice that they have felt bound by, and thereby find a route to their own unique and feminine expression. They do not operate within the gendered constraints of a patriarchal art world but create their own world of form and image, which may not be comfortable but which can be very beautiful. Both these sculptors show us something of vital importance—that female creativity can express itself through its own "hard art" and thereby be neither a copy, nor a subversion, of "masculine" artistic practice.

Those of us in the therapeutic professions would benefit greatly from nurturing dialogues with many other disciplines, not just the arts, so that our self-sustaining theories and ways of thinking are challenged and we are encouraged to "think outside the box". The world of the arts can teach us things about the human psyche that we may be blind to within the confines and languages of our own profession. Despite its enormous achievements, the therapeutic profession has created its own blind spots, by its insular and self-referencing theories and language. These blind spots have sustained and encouraged the abuses of the feminine prevalent in our cultures and our psyches and they have not encouraged, or sometimes not even been able to see, the multiple new possibilities for the feminine psyche to move into. Without this movement and growth we continue, men as well as women, to be impoverished.

REFERENCES

Abt, R., Bosch, I., & MacKrell, V. (2000). *Dream Child. Creation and New Life in Dreams of Pregnant Women.* Einsiedeln: Daimon Verlag.

Adams, T. (2003). Jung, Kristeva and the maternal realm. In: T. Adams & A. Duncan (Eds.), *The Feminine Case. Jung Aesthetics and Creative Process* (pp. 55–67). London: Karnac.

Allphin, C. (1999). Complexes and paradoxes in our organizational life. *Journal of Analytical Psychology, 44:* 249–258.

Angelo, M. (2003). "This thing of brightness": the feminine power of transcendent imagination. In: T. Adams & A. Duncan (Eds.), *The Feminine Case. Jung, Aesthetics and Creative Process* (pp. 119–146). London: Karnac.

Ankori, G. (2005). Frida Kahlo: the fabric of her art. In: E. Dexter & T. Barson (Eds.), *Frida Kahlo* (pp. 31–45). London: Tate.

Antich, X. (2004). Deconstructing the real, exploding the vision. In: *Cornelia Parker* (pp. 5–8). Barcelona: Galeria Carles Tache.

Austin, S. (1999). Women's aggressive fantasies. A feminist post-Jungian hermeneutic. *Harvest, 45*(2): 7–28.

Austin, S. (2005). *Women's Aggressive Fantasies. A Post-Jungian Exploration of Self-Hatred, Love and Agency.* London: Routledge.

Badinter, E. (1981). *The Myth of Motherhood. An Historical View of the Maternal Instinct.* London: Souvenir Press.

Bair, D. (2004). *Jung. A Biography.* London: Little Brown.

Balint, A. (1939). Love for the mother and mother-love. In: M. Balint (Ed.), *Primary Love and Psycho-Analytic Technique* (pp. 91–108). New York: Liverlight.

Balint, M. (1948). On the psychoanalytic training system. *International Journal of Psychoanalysis, 29*: 163–173.

Baring, A., & Cashford, J. (1993). *The Myth of the Goddess. Evolution of an Image*. Harmondsworth: Penguin Arkana.

Bernadec, M.-L. (1996). *Louise Bourgeois*. Paris: Flammarion.

Bollas, C. (2000). *Hysteria*. London: Routledge.

Bourgeois, L. (1998). *Louise Bourgeois. Destruction of the Father. Reconstruction of the Father. Writings and Interviews 1923–1997.* M.-L. Bernadec & H.-U. Obrist (Eds.). London: Violette Editions.

Bowlby, J. (1951). *Maternal Care and Mental Health*. The World Health Organisation.

Bruzzone, M., Casaula, E., Jimenez, J. P., & Jordan, J. F. (1985). Regression and persecution in analytic training. Reflections on experience. *International Review of Psychoanalysis, 12*: 411–414.

Bryan, E., & Higgins, R. (1995). *Infertility. New Choices. New Dilemmas*. London: Penguin.

Carpenter, R. (2005). *West Wing: Making Art and Architecture Work for Health*. London: Barts and the London NHS Trust.

Cheshire, N. M. (1996). The empire of the ear: Freud's problem with music. *International Journal of Psychoanalysis, 77*: 1127–1168.

Chodorow, N. J. (1999). *The Reproduction of Mothering*. London: University of California Press.

Christie, G. L., & Morgan, A. (2003). Love, hate and the generative couple. In: J. Haynes & J. Miller (Eds.), *Inconceivable Conceptions. Psychological Aspects of Infertility and Reproductive Technologies* (pp. 86–101). Hove: Brunner-Routledge.

Clark, M. (2003). Women's lack: the image of woman as divine. In: T. Adams & A. Duncan (Eds.), *The Feminine Case. Jung, Aesthetics and Creative Process* (pp. 185–203). London: Karnac.

Coltart, N. (1986). Slouching towards Bethlehem . . . or thinking the unthinkable in psychoanalysis. In: G. Kohon (Ed.), *The British School of Psychoanalysis. The Independent Tradition* (pp. 185–199). London: Free Association.

Cook, R. (1999). Critical essay. *Harvest, 45*(2): 144–153.

Culbert-Koehn, J. (2002). A Jungian view of the menopause: not for women only. *Harvest, 48*(1): 92–108.

Dally, A. (1982). *Inventing Motherhood: The Consequenses of an Ideal*. London: Burnett Books.

de Beauvoir, S. (1953). *The Second Sex*. London: Jonathan Cape.

Dexter, E., & Barson, T. (2005). *Frida Kahlo*. London: Tate.

Douglas, C. (1993). *Translate This Darkness. The Life of Christiana Morgan*. New York: Simon and Schuster.

Duncan, A. (2003a). The alchemy of inversion: Charlotte Brontë's *Jane Eyre* and Mary Kelly's "Menace". In: T. Adams & A. Duncan (Eds.), *The Feminine Case. Jung Aesthetics and Creative Process* (pp. 147–184). London: Karnac.

Duncan, A. (2003b). Individuation and necessity. In: T. Adams & A. Duncan (Eds.), *The Feminine Case. Jung, Aesthetics and Creative Process* (pp. 69–95). London: Karnac.

Duras, M. (1975). Smothered creativity. In: E. Marks & I. de Courtivron (Eds.), *New French Feminism*. New York: Schocken.

Finiello Zervas, D. (2003). Dark reflections. The shadow side of assisted reproductive techniques. In: J. Haynes & J. Miller (Eds.), *Inconceivable Conceptions. Psychological Aspects of Infertility and Reproductive Technology* (pp. 181–203). Hove: Brunner-Routledge.

Gabbard, G., & Lester, E. (1995). *Boundaries and Boundary Violations in Psychoanalysis*. Washington, DC: American Psychiatric Publishing.

Gerhardt, S. (2004). *Why Love Matters*. Hove: Brunner-Routledge.

Gerrard, N. (2001). Dealing with infertility. *Observer Magazine*, 14 January.

Gordon, R. (2000). *Dying and Creating. A Search for Meaning*. London: Karnac.

Gorovoy, J., & Asbaghi, P. T. (1997). *Louise Bourgeois. Blue Days and Pink Days*. Milan: Fondazione Prada.

Greer, G. (1979). *The Obstacle Race*. London: Secker and Warburg.

Hampton, C. (2002). *The Talking Cure*. London: Faber and Faber.

Harris, T. (1998). Outline of common benign lesions causing dysphonia. In: T. Harris, D. Harris, J. Rubin, & D. Howard (Eds.), *The Voice Clinic Handbook* (pp. 40–48). London: Whurr.

Haynes, J., & Miller, J. (2003). *Inconceivable Conceptions. Psychological Aspects of Infertility and Reproductive Technologies*. Hove: Brunner-Routledge.

Hillman, J. (1975). Betrayal. *Loose Ends*. Dallas, TX: Spring.

Hillman, J. (1992). *The Myth of Analysis*. Chicago, IL: Northwestern University Press.

Hubback, J. (1993). Eve: reflections on the psychology of the first disobedient woman. In: L. B. Ross (Ed.), *To Speak or Be Silent. The Paradox of Disobedience in the Lives of Women* (pp. 3–12). Wilmette, IL: Chiron.

Hustvedt, S. (2003). *What I Loved*. London: Hodder and Stoughton.

Jung, C. G. (1956). *Symbols of Transformation, CW, 5*. London: Routledge and Kegan Paul.

Jung, C. G. (1963). *Mysterium Coniunctionis. CW, 14*. London: Routledge and Kegan Paul.

Jung, C. G. (1996a). *The Psychology of Kundalini Yoga*. S. Shamdasani (Ed.). London: Routledge.

Jung, C. G. (1996b). *The Spirit in Man, Art and Literature. CW, 15*, Princeton, NJ: Princeton University Press: Bollingen Series XX.

Jung, C. G. (1997). *Visions: Notes of the Seminar Given in 1930–34*, Vol. 2. Clare Douglas (Ed.). Princeton, NJ: Princeton University Press.

Jung, C. G. (1982). *Aspects of the Feminine*. London: Ark Paperbacks.

Kennedy, H. (1993). *Eve was Framed. Women and British Justice*. London: Vintage.

Kernberg, O. F. (1986). Institutional problems of psychoanalytic education. *Journal of the American Psychoanalytic Association, 34*: 799–834.

Kernberg, O. F. (1996). Thirty methods to destroy the creativity of psychoanalytic candidates. *International Journal of Psychoanalysis, 77*: 1031–1040.

Kerr, J. (1994). *A Most Dangerous Method. The Story of Jung, Freud and Sabina Spielrein*. London: Sinclair-Stevenson.

Klein, M. (1988). *Envy and Gratitude and Other Works, 1946–1963*. London: Virago.

Koropatnick, S., Daniluk, J., & Pattinson, H. A. (1993). Infertility: a non-event transition. *Fertility and Sterility, 59*(1): 163–171.

Kradin, R. L. (1997). The psychosomatic symptom and the self: a siren's song. *Journal of Analytical Psychology, 42*(3): 405–423.

Kristeva, J. (1980). *Desire in Language. A Semiotic Approach to Literature and Art*. Oxford: Blackwell.

Leonard, L. S. (1998). *The Wounded Woman. Healing the Father–Daughter Relationship*. Boston, MA: Shambala.

Liotta, E. (1997). Animus and creativity in psychotherapy: a position statement. *Journal of Analytical Psychology, 42*(2): 317–324.

Maguire, M. (2004). *Men, Women, Passion and Power*. Hove: Brunner-Routledge.

Maiello, S. (1995). The sound-object: a hypothesis about prenatal auditory experience and memory. *Journal of Child Psychotherapy, 21*(1): 23–41.

Mantel, H. (2003). Clinical waste. In: J. Haynes & J. Miller (Eds.), *Inconceivable Conceptions. Psychological Aspects of Infertility and Reproductive Technology* (pp. 19–26). Hove: Brunner-Routledge.

Mariotti, P. (1997). Creativity and fertility: the one-parent phantasy. In:
  J. Raphael-Leff & R. Jozef Perelberg (Eds.), *Female Experience. Three
  Generations of British Women Psychoanalysts on Work with Women*.
  London: Routledge.

Marton, E. (2002). *Ich Hiess Sabina Spielrein*. Film.

McCormick, K. (1994). Sabina Spielrein. Biographical note and post-
  script. *Journal of Analytical Psychology, 39*: 187–190.

Miller, J. (2000). Training: fears of destruction and creativity. Reflections
  on the process of becoming an analyst. *Harvest, 46*(2): 53–69.

Miller, J. (2003). Mourning the never born and the loss of the angel. In:
  J. Haynes & J. Miller (Eds.), *Inconceivable Conceptions. Psychological
  Aspects of Infertility and Reproductive Technology* (pp. 47–59). Hove:
  Brunner-Routledge.

Milner, M. (1952). *A Life of One's Own*. London: Virago.

Moller, A., & Fallstrom, K. (1991). Psychological consequences of infertility: a longitudinal study. *Journal of Psychosomatic Obstetrics and
  Gynaecology, 12*: 27–45.

Morgan, C. (1938). Thematic apperception test. In: H. Murray (Ed.),
  *Explorations in Personality: A Clinical and Experimental Study of Fifty
  Men of College Age* (pp. 673–680). New York: Oxford University
  Press.

Morgan, C., & Murray, H. (1935). A method for investigating fantasies:
  the thematic apperception test. *Archives of Neurology and Psychiatry,
  34*: 289–306.

Morgan, C., & Murray, H. (1945). A clinical study of sentiments. *Genetic
  Psychology Monographs, 32*: 3–11.

Morgan, J. (2000). Matter and what it means. In: *Cornelia Parker*. Boston:
  The Institute of Contemporary Art.

Morris, F. (2003). *Louise Bourgeois. Stitches in Time*. London: August,
  IMMA.

Nin, A. (1973). *The Journals of Anais Nin*. Vol 1. London: Quartet.

Nin, A. (1975). *A Woman Speaks: The Lectures, Seminars and Interviews of
  Anais Nin*. E. J. Hinz, (Ed.). Chicago, IL: Swallow Press.

Oucharenko, V. (1999). Love, psychoanalysis and destruction. *Journal of
  Analytical Psychology, 44*(3): 355–373.

Parker, C. (2000). Cornelia Parker interviewed by Bruce Ferguson. In:
  Cornelia Parker. Boston, MA: The Institute of Contemporary Art.

Parker, C. (2001a). Caption to "Breathless". The Victoria and Albert
  Museum, London.

Parker, C. (2001b). Anarchy and ecstasy. *Economist*, 9 June.

Parker, C. (2004). Interview with J. Miller. 12 July.

Parker, R. (1995). *Torn in Two. The Experience of Maternal Ambivalence.* London: Virago.

Parker, R., & Pollock, G. (1987). *Framing Feminism: Art and the Women's Movement 1970–1985.* London: Pandora.

Pattis Zoja, E. (1997). *Abortion. Loss and Renewal in the Search for Identity.* London: Routledge.

Piontelli, A. (1987). Infant observation from before birth. *International Journal of Psychoanalysis, 68*: 453–463.

Piontelli, A. (1992). *From Foetus to Child: An Observational and Psychoanalytic Study.* London: Brunner Routledge.

Pfeffer, N. (1987). Artificial insemination, in-vitro fertilization and the stigma of infertility. In: M. Stanworth (Ed.), *Reproductive Technologies. Gender, Motherhood and Medicine* (pp. 81–97). Cambridge: Polity Press.

Pines, D. (1993). *A Woman's Unconscious Use of Her Body.* London: Virago.

Raphael-Leff, J. (1985). Fear and fantasies of childbirth. *Journal of Pre and Perinatal Psychology, 1*: 14–18.

Reeder, J. (2004). *Hate and Love in Psychoanalytic Institutions. The Dilemma of a Profession.* New York: Other Press.

Rich, A. (1977). *Of Woman Born.* London: Virago.

Ross, L. B. (1993). Introduction. In: *To Speak or Be Silent. The Paradox of Disobedience in the Lives of Women* (pp. xi–xxiv). Wilmette, IL: Chiron.

Rousseau, J. J. (1902). *Emile.* London: Edward Arnold.

Rowland, S. (2002). *Jung. A Feminist Revision.* Cambridge: Polity Press.

Sacks, O. (2001). *Uncle Tungsten. Memories of a Chemical Boyhood.* London: Picador.

Sage, L. (2000). *Bad Blood. A Memoir.* London: Fourth Estate.

Samuels, A. (1981). Fragmentary vision: a central training aim. *Spring,* 215–225.

Samuels, A. (1993). *The Political Psyche.* London: Routledge.

Samuels, A., Shorter, B., & Plaut, F. (1986). *A Critical Dictionary of Jungian Analysis.* London: Routledge and Kegan Paul.

Shearer, A. (1996). *Athene. Image and Energy.* Harmondsworth: Penguin Arkana.

Shewell, C. (2002). Personal communication.

Sinason, V. (2002). *Attachment, Trauma and Multiplicity: Working with Dissociative Identity Disorder.* London: Routledge,

Spielrein, S. (1994). Destruction as the cause of coming into being. *Journal of Analytical Psychology, 39*:155–185.

Spurling, H. (2005). *Matisse. The Master.* London: Hamish Hamilton.

Taylor, D. (2004). One baby equals two unwritten books *Mslexia, 23*: 10–13.

Ulanov, A. B. (2001). *Receiving Woman.* Einsiedeln: Daimon Verlag.

Winnicott, D. W. (1992a). Primary maternal preoccupation. In: *Through Paediatrics to Psychoanalysis* (pp. 300–305). London: Karnac.

Winnicott, D. W. (1992b) Aggression in relation to emotional development. In: *Through Paediatrics to Psychoanalysis* (pp. 204–218). London: Karnac.

Wolff, T. (1956). Structural forms of the feminine psyche. P. Watzlawick (Trans.). Zurich: Student's Association of the C. G. Jung Institute.

Woolf, V. (1945). *A Room of One's Own.* Harmondsworth: Penguin.

Woodman, M. (1985). *The Pregnant Virgin. A Process of Psychological Transformation.* Toronto: Inner City Books.

Woodman, M. (1992). *Leaving My Father's House. A Journey to Conscious Femininity.* London: Shambhala.

Wollstonecraft, M. (1975). *Vindication of the Rights of Woman.* Harmondsworth: Penguin.

Young-Eisendrath, P. (2004). *Subject to Change. Jung Gender and Subjectivity in Psychoanalysis.* Hove: Brunner-Routledge.

INDEX